Editor
Mary S. Jones, M.A.

Illustrator
Kelly McMahon

Cover Artist
Barb Lorseyedi

Managing Editor
Ina Massler Levin, M.A.

Creative Director
Karen J. Goldfluss, M.S. Ed.

Art Production Manager
Kevin Barnes

Art Coordinator
Renée Christine Yates

Imaging
Leonard P. Swierski
Nathan P. Rivera
James Edward Grace

Publisher
Mary D. Smith, M.S. Ed.

FLIPPING OVER
MAKING WORDS

wish

w i sh

mesh

_sh

Author

Jessica M. Dubin Kissel, M.A.

Teacher Created Resources, Inc.
6421 Industry Way
Westminster, CA 92683
www.teachercreated.com
ISBN: 978-1-4206-8616-6
© 2007 Teacher Created Resources, Inc.
Made in U.S.A.

Teacher Created Resources

Table of Contents

Table of Contents *(cont.)*

Introduction

Flipping Over Making Words is a supplemental series designed for helping emergent readers. Templates are provided for teachers to make student flip books to actively show how words can be manipulated by changing a letter or series of letters.

Flip books provide a wonderful opportunity to tap into kinesthetic learners. Kinesthetic learners will thrive as they get to use their hands to flip pages in order to make words. Flip books also allow students to make words without the frustrations that are connected with writing words using pencil and paper. Furthermore, flip books give every student the opportunity to be actively involved in making words at the same time.

Following each flip book is a word list, activity ideas for teachers, and student handouts. The activities were written to be age appropriate and to help develop students' reading and writing skills. Best of all, these activities are meant to be motivational and fun.

Teachers can use the materials provided, create their own activities using the flip books and word lists, or simply call out words on the list and ask the students to make those words.

This series is not a reading program; this series was designed so that teachers can pull active and interesting activities into their lessons as instructional aids and as follow-up practice. Teachers should not feel like they need to use the activities in any particular order.

Variations on Making Flip Books

Templates are provided so that teachers can easily make flip books for students using just paper, scissors, and staples. However, there are other ways that the flip books can be made and used in the classroom:

- Make a flip book for a group of students to use together.

- Make one large flip book to use as a class.

- Use rings or plastic spiral binders instead of staples.

- Once the flip book is stapled, separate the different columns so that the flip book is no longer one unit. Have different students be responsible for different parts of the flip book.

- Use different colors of paper.

- Put a row of blank squares on the top of the flip book. Have the students illustrate them.

- Laminate the flip books or use cardstock to make them sturdy.

- Have the students cut out their own flip books to develop fine motor skills.

- Distribute blank flip books and have the students fill in the letters using their own writing.

- Have students trace the letters with glue and add glitter.

Cautionary Note: Please be advised that while using the flip books, there is always the possibility that undesirable or unexpected words can be formed. Such words are not included in the word lists.

Standards and Benchmarks

Listed below are the McREL standards for Languange Arts, Level 1 (grades K–2). All standards and benchmarks are used with permission from McREL.

Kendall, J. S., & Marzano R. J. (2004). *Content knowledge: A compendium of standards and benchmarks for K–12 education.* Aurora, CO: Mid-continent Research for Education and Learning. Online database:

http://www.mcrel.org/standards-benchmarks/

McREL Standards are in **bold**. Benchmarks are in regular print. The ideas and activities throughout this book meet the following standards and benchmarks. The page numbers for the correlating handouts are listed to the right.

3. Uses grammatical and mechanical conventions in written compositions

Uses conventions of print in writing (e.g., forms letters in print, uses upper- and lowercase letters of the alphabet, spaces words and sentences, writes from left-to-right and top-to-bottom)	18, 26, 27, 37, 38, 41, 50, 51, 52, 53, 54, 64, 66, 67, 85, 86, 88, 89, 90, 91, 92, 96, 97, 106, 109, 110, 111, 119, 120, 121, 122, 123, 131, 132, 133, 136, 144, 145, 146, 152, 153, 154, 160, 161, 162, 167, 169, 171, 172
Uses verbs in written compositions (e.g., verbs for a variety of situations, action words)	169, 170, 171, 172
Uses conventions of spelling in written compositions (e.g., spells high frequency, commonly misspelled words from appropriate grade-level list; spells phonetically regular words; uses letter-sound relationships; spells basic short vowel, long vowel, r-controlled, and consonant blend patterns)	18, 26, 27, 37, 38, 41, 50, 51, 52, 53, 54, 64, 66, 67, 85, 86, 88, 89, 90, 91, 92, 96, 97, 106, 109, 110, 111, 119, 120, 121, 122, 123, 131, 132, 133, 136, 144, 145, 146, 152, 153, 154, 160, 161, 162, 167, 169, 171, 172

5. Uses the general skills and strategies of the reading process

Uses basic elements of phonetic analysis (e.g., common letter/sound relationships, beginning and ending consonants, vowel sounds, blends, word patterns) to decode unknown words	All student handouts
Uses basic elements of structural analysis (e.g., syllables, basic prefixes, suffixes, root words, spelling patterns) to decode unknown words	All student handouts
Understands level-appropriate sight words and vocabulary (e.g., words for persons, places, things, actions; high frequency words such as *said*, *was*, and *where*)	All student handouts

8. Uses listening and speaking strategies for different purposes

Makes contributions in class and group discussions (e.g., initiates conversations, connects ideas and experiences with those of others)	16, 18, 39, 50, 65, 93, 94, 95, 107, 119, 134, 135, 144, 145
Asks and responds to questions (e.g., about the meaning of a story, about the meaning of words or ideas)	16, 18, 50, 65, 119, 134, 135, 144, 145
Follows rules of conversation and group discussion (e.g., takes turns, raises hand to speak, stays on topic, focuses attention on speaker)	16, 18, 50, 65, 93, 94, 95, 119, 134, 135, 144, 145, 169, 170
Uses different voice level, phrasing, and intonation for different situations (e.g., small group settings, informal discussions, reports to the class)	18, 65, 93, 94, 95, 119, 144, 145, 152, 160, 169, 170
Uses level-appropriate vocabulary in speech (e.g., number words; words that describe people, places, things, events, location, actions; synonyms, antonyms; homonyms)	16, 18, 39, 50, 93, 94, 95, 107, 119, 134, 135, 144, 145
Gives and responds to oral directions	All student handouts

Short Vowels Flip Book

Directions: Make a flip book for each student.

1. Copy pages 6–11.

2. Cut out the strips along the outside dashed lines.

3. Cut the boxes vertically, cutting only on the dashed lines. Make sure not to cut on the solid lines.

4. Stack the strips on top of each other and staple them together where the staple marks are indicated.

staple	staple	staple
b	a	b

staple	staple	staple
c	e	d

Short Vowels Flip Book (cont.)

staple	staple	staple
d	i	g

staple	staple	staple
f	o	l

staple	staple	staple
g	u	m

Short Vowels Flip Book *(cont.)*

staple	staple	staple
h		n

staple	staple	staple
j		p

staple	staple	staple
l		r

Short Vowels Flip Book *(cont.)*

staple	staple	staple
m		s

staple	staple	staple
n		t

staple	staple	staple
p		x

Short Vowels Flip Book *(cont.)*

staple	staple	staple
r		

staple	staple	staple
s		

staple	staple	staple
t		

Short Vowels Flip Book *(cont.)*

staple	staple	staple
w		

staple	staple	staple
y		

Short Vowels Word List

Listed below are some words that can be made using the Short Vowels Flip Book.
Note: Although the words in *italics* can be made with the flip book, they will not be pronounced with a short vowel sound.

bad	can	fan	ham	lab	map	pan	rat	tab	tax
bag	cap	fax	has	lad	nag	pat	sad	tag	wag
ban	*car*	gap	hat	lap	nap	rag	sag	tan	*was*
bat	cat	gas	jam	mad	pad	ram	sap	tap	wax
cab	dad	had	*jar*	man	pal	ran	sat	*tar*	yam

bed	fed	hem	leg	net	red	wet
beg	gel	hen	let	peg	set	yes
bet	gem	jet	men	pen	ten	yet
den	get	led	met	pet	web	

bib	did	fin	him	lid	mix	pit	rip	tin
big	dig	fit	hip	jig	nip	rib	sip	tip
bin	dip	fix	his	lip	pig	rig	sit	win
bit	fig	hid	hit	lit	pin	rim	six	wig

bob	cop	fog	hop	log	mop	pop	rot
bog	cot	fox	hot	lot	nod	pot	sob
box	dog	got	job	mob	not	rob	*son*
cob	dot	hog	jog	mom	pod	rod	top

bud	but	dug	hum	mud	rub	tub
bug	cub	fun	hut	mug	rug	tug
bun	cup	gum	jug	nut	run	yum
bus	cut	hug	lug	pup	sun	

Activity Ideas for Teachers

The following activities can be used with the Short Vowels Flip Book. Many of the activities have supporting materials. The page numbers where the materials can be found are provided.

Flipping Over Animals

Directions

1. Cut out and separate the pictures of the animals (page 17).
2. Place students into pairs or groups, or have them work individually.
3. Hold up a picture of an animal for the students to see.
4. Have students use their flip books to identify the animals that they see.
5. Have students hold up their flip books to show you the word that they made.
6. Continue until you have shown the students each of the pictures.

Extension Idea: You may want to give students their own copies of the different animals and have them color in the pictures. Encourage them to write the names of the animals next to the pictures using their flip books as a guide to help them make the words.

Answer Key:

1. fox	2. hen	3. bat	4. cat	5. rat	6. pig

Short Vowels Groups

Directions

1. Break the class up into five groups and number each group 1–5.
2. Assign each group one short vowel sound.
3. Distribute copies of the handout that matches their assigned vowel sound (pages 18–22).
4. Have each group make three words that have their assigned vowel sound using their flip books.
5. Have the groups record their words in their group's box on the handout.
6. Reassign the vowels to different groups. Redistribute the handouts to the appropriate groups.
7. Instruct each group to try to come up with three new words to add to the list.
8. Continue until each group has had a turn to work with each vowel.

Answer Key: Answers will vary. Use the Short Vowels Word List on page 12 for possible answers.

Activity Ideas for Teachers *(cont.)*

Moving Letters

Directions

1. Copy and cut out the word cards on pages 23–25.
2. Hold up the first word (*bat*) for the students to see.
3. Have the students use their flip books to make the same word.
4. Have the students read the word.
5. Continue until you have shown the students all of the words, making sure to go in numbered order.

Note: Explain to the students that they only need to change ONE letter in order to make the new word.

A-E-I-O-U

Directions

1. Distribute copies of the handout on page 26.
2. Instruct the students to use their flip books to help them make words to describe the pictures on the page.
3. Tell the students that the short vowels *a*, *e*, *i*, *o*, and *u* will be used only once to complete this worksheet.
4. Then place the students in pairs and have the students practice reading the words that they made.

Answer Key:

1. hat   2. net   3. bib   4. pot   5. mug

More A-E-I-O-U

Directions

1. Distribute copies of the handout on page 27.
2. Instruct the students to use their flip books to help them make words to describe the pictures on the page.
3. Tell the students that the short vowels *a*, *e*, *i*, *o*, and *u* will be used only once to complete this worksheet.
4. Then place the students in pairs and have the students practice reading the words that they made.

Answer Key:

1. fan   2. bed   3. lid   4. box   5. nut

Activity Ideas for Teachers *(cont.)*

Say and Show

Directions

1. Only the letters *a, e, i, o,* and *u* will be used for this activity. Either have the students separate their flip books so that they are only holding the middle (vowel) section, tell the students to only focus on the middle section, or paperclip the two end sections so that students can only manipulate the middle (vowel) section.

2. Tell the students to listen carefully for the vowel sound as you read some words aloud.

3. Have your students identify the letter of the vowel sound, find that letter in their flip books, and hold up the letter for you to see.

   A suggested list of words is provided below for you to read. For more words to read, you can use the Short Vowels Word List on page 12.

bag	bug	fin	set	sob	top
bit	bed	fan	sip	hat	gem
bus	box	fun	sat	wig	bun

Silly Word, Silly Dance

Directions

1. Ask each student to select one letter from each column of their flip book.

2. Model for the students what you want them to do. Share the three letters that you selected. For example, you might select *b-a-b*.

3. Explain that each person will have a chance to read the letters that he or she picked. (As they read, they will need to remember to use the short vowel sounds.)

4. Read your example to the students. Say, "bab."

5. Then, explain that if the letters that they picked make a real word, everyone should clap their hands. But, if the letters make a silly word, like *bab*, everyone should do a silly dance at their seats instead.

6. In turn, have the students read their "words." Help the class decide if the word is real or silly.

Activity Ideas for Teachers *(cont.)*

Riddles with Short Vowel Sounds

Directions

1. Have the students work individually, in pairs, or in groups.
2. Read the riddles aloud in the order that they appear below. The answers are designed so that only one letter needs to change in order to solve the riddle. Point this out to the students.
3. Have the students make the word that solves the riddle using their flip books.
4. Have the students hold up their flip books to show you their solutions to the riddle.
5. Make sure all of the students have the correct answer before moving on to the next riddle.
6. Continue until all of the riddles have been read.

Read the following riddles:

1. I am a color on the American Flag. I am not blue or white.
   Answer: *red*
2. You sleep on this at night.
   Answer: *bed*
3. I am the opposite of good.
   Answer: *bad*
4. I help you to hold things, like trash or groceries.
   Answer: *bag*
5. I am the opposite of small.
   Answer: *big*
6. You can do this in sand, snow, and dirt.
   Answer: *dig*
7. You use this to add extra flavor to chips and vegetables.
   Answer: *dip*
8. I am a body part. (Point to your hip.)
   Answer: *hip*
9. What I am doing. (Demonstrate a hop.)
   Answer: *hop*
10. I am the opposite of bottom.
    Answer: *top*

Flipping Over Animals

Directions: Cut out the animal cards along the dashed lines.

1.

2.

3.

4.

5.

6.

Short Vowels Groups

Directions: With your group, use your flip books to make three new words using the short *a* sound. Write your words in your group's box below.

Group 1

___ a ___   ___ a ___   ___ a ___

Group 2

___ a ___   ___ a ___   ___ a ___

Group 3

___ a ___   ___ a ___   ___ a ___

Group 4

___ a ___   ___ a ___   ___ a ___

Group 5

___ a ___   ___ a ___   ___ a ___

Short Vowels Groups *(cont.)*

Directions: With your group, use your flip books to make three new words using the short *e* sound. Write your words in your group's box below.

Group 1

___ e ___   ___ e ___   __ e ___

Group 2

___ e ___   ___ e ___   ___ e ___

Group 3

___ e ___   ___ e ___   ___ e ___

Group 4

___ e ___   ___ e ___   ___ e ___

Group 5

___ e ___   __ e ___   __ e ___

Short Vowels Groups *(cont.)*

Directions: With your group, use your flip books to make three new words using the short *i* sound. Write your words in your group's box below.

Group 1

___ i ___   ___ i ___   ___ i ___

Group 2

___ i ___   ___ i ___   ___ i ___

Group 3

___ i ___   ___ i ___   ___ i ___

Group 4

___ i ___   ___ i ___   ___ i ___

Group 5

___ i ___   ___ i ___   ___ i ___

Short Vowels Groups *(cont.)*

Directions: With your group, use your flip books to make three new words using the short *o* sound. Write your words in your group's box below.

Group 1

___ O ___   ___ O ___   ___ O ___

Group 2

___ O ___   ___ O ___   ___ O ___

Group 3

___ O ___   ___ O ___   ___ O ___

Group 4

___ O ___   ___ O ___   ___ O ___

Group 5

___ O ___   ___ O ___   ___ O ___

Short Vowels Groups *(cont.)*

Directions: With your group, use your flip books to make three new words using the short *u* sound. Write your words in your group's box below.

Group 1

___ U ___   ___ U ___   ___ U

Group 2

___ U ___   ___ U ___   ___ U

Group 3

___ U ___   ___ U ___   ___ U

Group 4

___ U ___   ___ U ___   ___ U

Group 5

___ U ___   ___ U ___   ___ U

Moving Letters

Directions: Before class, cut out the following word cards along the dashed lines.

1.

bat

2.

bet

3.

bit

4.

fit

Moving Letters *(cont.)*

5.

fin

6.

fun

7.

run

8.

ran

9.

pan

Moving Letters *(cont.)*

10.

pin

11.

pen

12.

ten

13.

tan

A-E-I-O-U

Directions: Use your flip book to help you make a word to describe each picture.

1.

_____

2.

_____

3.

_____

4.

_____

5.

_____

More A-E-I-O-U

Directions: Use your flip book to help you make a word to describe each picture.

1.

2.

3.

4.

5.
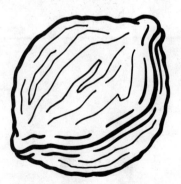

Long Vowels and Silent E Flip Book

Directions: Make a flip book for each student.

1. Copy pages 28–31.
2. Cut out the strips along the outside dashed lines.
3. Cut the boxes vertically, cutting only on the dashed lines. Make sure not to cut on the solid lines.
4. Stack the strips on top of each other and staple them together where the staple marks are indicated.

Note: Have the students color in each letter *e* with a colored pencil. Remind them that the letter *e* at the end of a word is usually silent. The letter *e* at the end of a word can make the vowel in the middle of the word say its name.

staple	staple	staple
b	a	e

staple	staple	staple
c	e	be

Long Vowels and Silent E Flip Book *(cont.)*

staple	staple	staple
f	i	ce

staple	staple	staple
h	o	de

staple	staple	staple
l	u	ke

Long Vowels and Silent E Flip Book (cont.)

staple	staple	staple
m		le

staple	staple	staple
n		me

staple	staple	staple
r		ne

Long Vowels and Silent E Flip Book *(cont.)*

staple	staple	staple
s		pe

staple	staple	staple
t		te

staple	staple	staple
w		ve

Long Vowels and Silent E Word List

Listed below are some words that can be made using the Long Vowels and Silent E Flip Book.

bake	face	lake	mane	sake	tale
cake	fade	lame	mate	sale	tape
came	fake	late	name	same	tame
cane	fame	made	race	sane	wade
cape	hate	make	rake	save	wake
cave	lace	male	rate	take	wave

bee	fee	see	tee

bike	five	lice	mice	nine	side	time
bite	hide	like	mile	rice	site	wide
file	hike	lime	mine	ride	tide	wipe
fine	hive	line	nice	ripe	tile	

bone	cove	hole	mole	rode	sole	tote
code	foe	home	mope	role	toe	woke
cone	hoe	hope	robe	rope	tone	wove

cube	cute	mule	rude	sue	tune
cue	fume	mute	rule	tube	

Activity Ideas for Teachers

The following activities can be used with the Long Vowels and Silent E Flip Book. All of the activities have supporting materials. The page numbers where the materials can be found are provided.

=========================== **The Long A Tale** ===========================

Directions: Before class, cut out the signal card (page 36). You will need this card for Part II of the activity.

Part I

1. Read *Nate and the Magic Cape* aloud to the class (below). Have the students listen for the long *a* sound as you read the story. Have them wave their flip books in the air every time they hear the long *a* sound.

2. Discuss any words or concepts in the story that you feel your students might not understand. For example, you might want to discuss the words *male, sugar cane,* etc.

Part II

1. Place your students in pairs or groups, or have them work individually.

2. Reread the story. This time as you read, have the students use their flip books to make some long *a* words. Explain the following activity to your students:

   A. Listen as I read the story.

   B. When I hold up this signal card (hold up the card for students to see), I want you to use your flip books to make the word that I say.

   C. Once you feel that you have made the word correctly, hold up your flip books so that I can see the word.

Some suggested words for the students to make are in bold. Teachers may ask their students to make more or fewer words, depending on their students' skills (as not all long *a* words are marked).

Nate and the Magic Cape

Once there was a **male** named Nate, who decided he was going to **bake** a **cake**. He baked the cake with sugar **cane**. He stayed up **late** to make it great. As the moon began to wane, he realized that it had gotten too late. He would not get to finish baking his cake unless . . .

Deep into his **cave** Nate did wade, across the lake he did race. Nate began to search for his magic **cape**, his special cape that he saved for when his energy began to **fade**. He found his cape and went back home. He still needed to finish making that **same** cake. He waved his cape, and nothing happened. He waved it again, and again nothing happened.

"I hate to admit it," Nate did say, "but I think my magic cape is a **fake**." So, the very same day, Nate washed the flour off of his face. He went to the store and bought a cake that was already made.

Activity Ideas for Teachers *(cont.)*

Rhyme Time with the Long I

Directions

1. Place your students in pairs or groups, or have them work individually. Distribute copies of the handout on page 37 accordingly.

2. Explain that they will be using their flip books to make words that rhyme.

3. Instruct your students to place the middle column of their flip books on the letter *i* and the last column of their flip books on the letters *de*.

4. Have the students flip through the first column of their flip books in order to find rhyming words.

5. Have students record their words on the handout.

6. Continue with the activity, instructing the students to change the middle and last columns of their flip books to form the following letter combinations:

   -ide, *-ine*, *-ice*, *-ike*, and *-ile*.

Answer Key: Answers may include:

hide,	wide,	side	
fine,	line,	mine,	nine
lice,	mice,	nice,	rice
bike,	hike,	like	
file,	mile,	tile	

O, Can You Finish That Word?

Directions

1. Distribute copies of the handout on page 38.

2. Explain to the students that they should use their flip books to help them finish making the words on their handouts. They should use the pictures provided to help them.

Answer Key:

1. toe	3. bone	5. rope
2. robe	4. cone	6. home

Activity Ideas for Teachers *(cont.)*

Can "U" Guess It?

Directions

1. Before class, copy and cut out each of the illustrations on pages 39–40.

2. Number the back of each illustration as numbered on the front. The same numbers are provided in the answer key below. This will help you figure out which word matches which illustration.

3. Place the illustrations facedown on a wall so that the students cannot see them.

4. Have the students work in pairs, groups, or individually. Have them use their flip books to see how many words they can make that have the long *u* vowel sound.

5. When a student makes a word, have him or her hold up the word. If the word is correct, turn over the illustration that matches the word so that the students can see it.

6. Continue the activity until the students have uncovered each illustration.

Answer Key:

1. cute	3. cube	5. rude	7. rule	9. fume
2. mute	4. tube	6. mule	8. tune	10. cue

Hungry Mice

Directions

1. Distribute copies of the handout on page 41.

2. Instruct the students to use their flip books to help them complete the words inside the pictures of the mice and the cheese.

3. Then have the students draw a line connecting the words that have the same long vowel sounds.

4. Place students into pairs and have them practice reading the words that they made.

Answer Key: Answers will vary. Use the Silent E Word List on page 32 for possible answers.

Ice Cream Sundae

Directions

1. Distribute copies of the handout on page 42.

2. Instruct the students to use their flip books to help them complete the words inside the ice cream sundae.

3. Then place students into pairs or into groups and have them read the words that they made.

Answer Key: Answers will vary. Use the Silent E Word List on page 32 for possible answers.

The Long A Tale

Directions: Cut out the following signal card along the dashed lines.

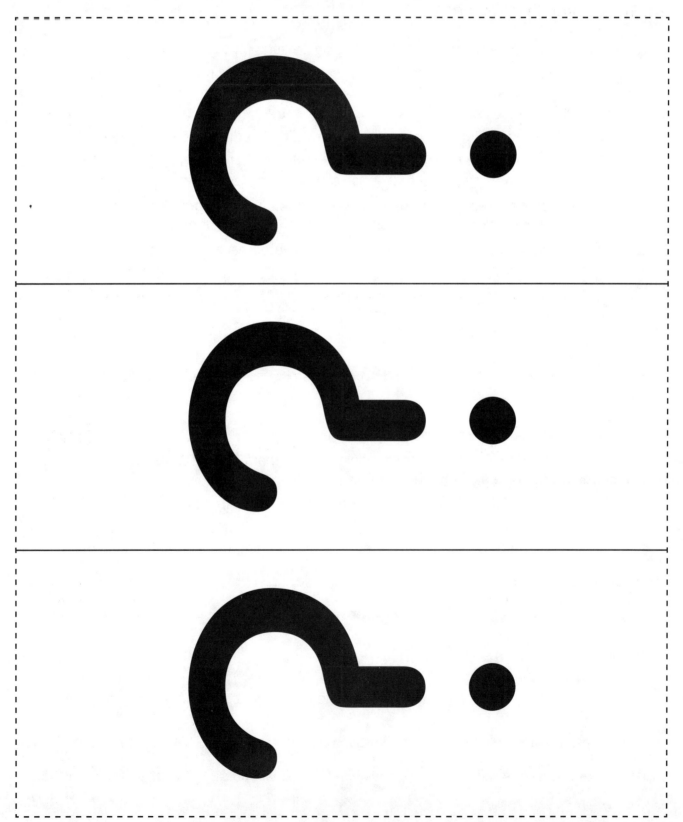

36

Rhyme Time with the Long I

Directions: Use your flip book to help you make rhyming words. Write down the rhyming words that you find.

_____ ide   _____ ide   _____ ide

_____ ine   _____ ine   _____ ine

_____ ice   _____ ice   _____ ice

_____ ike   _____ ike   _____ ike

_____ ile   _____ ile   _____ ile

O, Can You Finish That Word?

Directions: Use your flip book to help you find the correct ending to each word. Write the ending of each word on the lines. Use the pictures to help you.

1. to_____

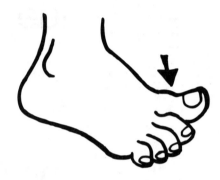

2. ro_____

3. bo_____

4. co_____

5. ro_____

6. ho_____

Can "U" Guess It?

Directions: Before class, cut out the following cards and number them as instructed on page 35.

1.

cute

2.

mute

3.

cube

4.

tube

Can "U" Guess It? *(cont.)*

5. rude

6. mule

7. 1. No running. 2. Be quiet.
rule

8. tune

9. fume

10. Action!
cue

Long Vowels and Silent E

Hungry Mice

Directions: Use your flip book to help you finish the words inside the mice and inside the cheese. Then draw a line connecting each mouse to the cheese that has the same long vowel sound.

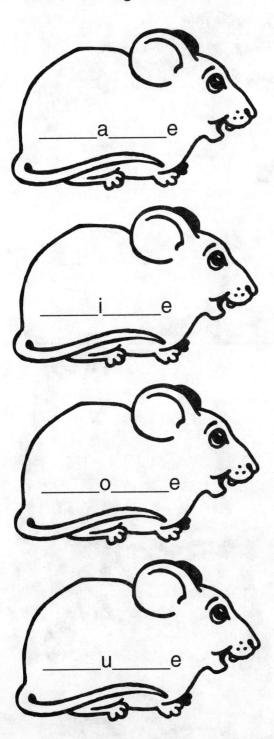

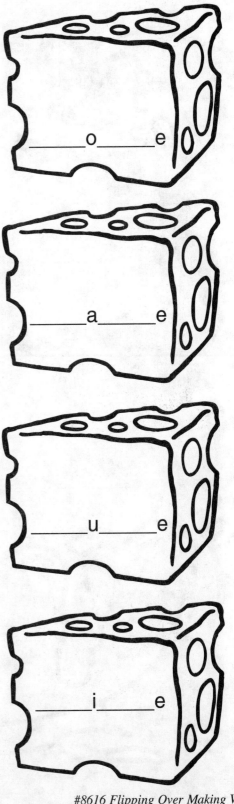

Ice Cream Sundae

Directions: Use your flip book to help you finish the words inside the scoops of ice cream.

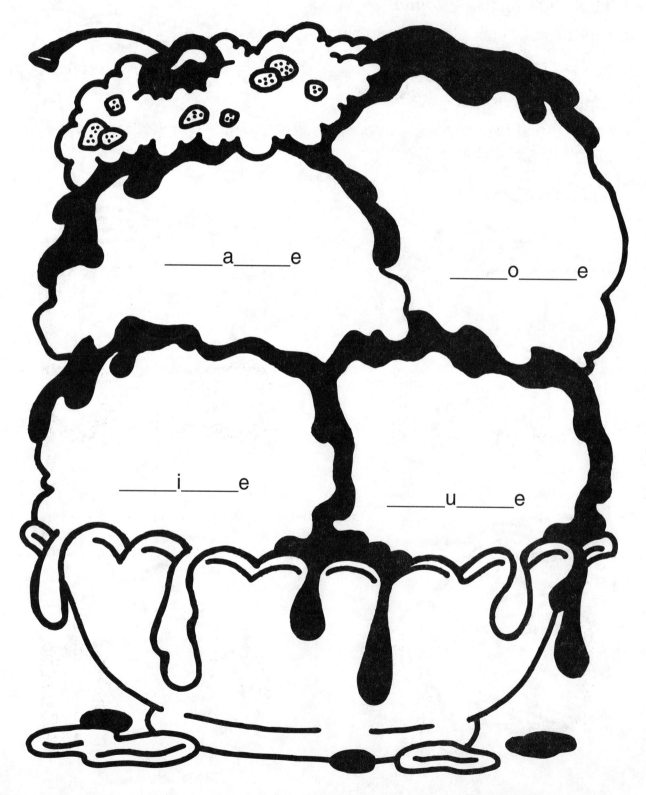

____a____e

____o____e

____i____e

____u____e

Beginning Letter Blends Flip Book

Directions: Make a flip book for each student.

1. Copy pages 43–45.

2. Cut out the strips along the outside dashed lines.

3. Cut the boxes vertically, cutting only on the dashed lines. Make sure not to cut on the solid lines.

4. Stack the strips on top of each other and staple them together where the staple marks are indicated.

staple	staple	staple	staple
c	l	a	d

staple	staple	staple	staple
b	p	e	g

Beginning Letter Blends Flip Book *(cont.)*

staple	staple	staple	staple
d	r	i	m

staple	staple	staple	staple
f	t	o	n

staple	staple	staple	staple
g		u	p

Beginning Letter Blends Flip Book (cont.)

staple	staple	staple	staple
p			t

staple	staple	staple	staple
s			w

staple	staple	staple	staple
t			

Beginning Letter Blends Word List

Listed below are some words that can be made using the Beginning Letter Blends Flip Book.

clam
clap
claw
clip
clog
clot

tram
trap
trim
trip
trod
trot

gram
grew
grid
grim
grin
grip
grit
grow

fret
frog
from

drag
draw
drew
drip
drop
drug
drum

cram
crew
crop
crow
crud

plan
plot
plow
plug
plum

spam
span
spat
sped
spin
spit
spot
spud
spun

glad
glow
glum

slam
slap
sled
slid
slim
slip
slit
slop
slot
slow
slug

stag
stem
step
stew
stop
stow
stud
stun

flag
flap
flat
flaw
fled
flew
flip
flop
flow

brag
bran
brat
brew
brig
brim
brow

Activity Ideas for Teachers

The following activities can be used with the Beginning Letter Blends Flip Book. All of the activities have supporting materials. The page numbers where the materials can be found are provided.

Crossword Puzzler

Directions

1. Distribute copies of the crossword puzzle on page 50.

2. Work together with your students to solve the puzzle. Read the clues aloud to the class.

3. Have your students use their flip books to try to find the correct answers.

4. When the students have found the correct answers, have them hold up their flip books for you to see.

5. Once you have checked that their answers are correct, help the students write the answers on the crossword puzzle. You may want to use a transparency of page 50 to help students write in the correct boxes.

Answer Key:

Across

  1. flap

  3. spit

  4. trap

  5. clap

Down

  1. flop

  2. trip

  3. spot

1. f	l	a	p		2. t		3. s	p	i	t
l				4. t	r	a	p			
o					i		o			
p		5. c	l	a	p		t			

Activity Ideas for Teachers *(cont.)*

Just One More!

Directions

1. Distribute copies of the handout on page 51.

2. Together with the students, read the words that are on the page.

3. Then using their flip books, have students work individually, in groups, or in pairs to find just one more word that begins with the same consonant blend as the first word given.

Answer Key: Answers may include:

1. flag, flat, flaw, fled, flew, flip, flop, flow
2. cram, crew, crow, crud
3. tram, trap, trim, trip, trod
4. spam, span, spat, sped, spin, spit, spud, spun
5. clap, claw, clip, clog, clot
6. brag, bran, brat, brew, brig, brim
7. grew, grid, grim, grin, grip, grit, grow
8. plot, plow, plug, plum
9. slam, slap, slid, slim, slip, slit, slop, slot, slow, slug
10. drag, draw, drew, drip, drop, drug

Switching Letters

Directions

1. Distribute copies of the handout on page 52.
2. Have students work in groups, pairs, or individually to complete the handout.
3. Instruct students to use their flip books to help them make a new word by changing one letter in each set of words.
4. Complete the first set of words together as a class. Show the students how you can use your flip book to change the word *glow* to *blow*, *flow*, *slow*, or *plow*.

Answer Key: Answers may vary. Use the Beginning Letter Blends Word List on page 46 for possible answers.

Talk

Directions

1. Distribute copies of the handout on page 53.
2. Have the students work in groups, pairs, or individually.
3. Read the first part of each conversation aloud to the students. Have them use their flip books to help them fill in the missing letters in each conversation.

Answer Key:

1. drew   2. flew   3. grew   4. spun

Activity Ideas for Teachers *(cont.)*

Winter Words

Directions

1. Distribute copies of the handout on page 54.

2. Help the students complete the words in each snowflake by reading aloud a series of clues for each word. Winter Word Clues are provided below and on page 54.

3. When students have identified the correct word, have them make the word using their flip books and hold up their flip books so that you can see the word.

4. Once you have checked that the letters are correct, have the students fill in the answers on their handouts.

Winter Word Clues

1. Walk carefully on icy surfaces so you do not do this. This word can be found in the word *slipper*. You wear this under a thin skirt.

2. In the snow, you can ride on this down hills. This object has runners to help it slide. Dogs are sometimes used to pull these objects over ice.

3. This hot dish is a thick soup. Ingredients might contain carrots, beef, and potatoes.

4. This vehicle moves snow off roads and parking lots. This vehicle has a large shovel on its front.

Answer Key:

1. slip

2. sled

3. stew

4. plow

Crossword Puzzler

Directions: Complete the crossword puzzle using the clues below and your flip book to help you.

Across

1. what birds do with their wings in the air

3. what you do to watermelon seeds

4. something people set to catch animals

5. what you do at the end of a performance to show how much you enjoyed it

Down

1. what you don't want to do in the water: a belly _____

2. another word for *vacation*

3. something black on a Dalmatian dog

Just One More!

Directions: Find just one more word that starts with the same letters as the given word. Use your flip book to help you. An example has been done for you.

stop   stem

1. flap ➜ fl _____   6. brow ➜ br _____

2. crop ➜ cr _____   7. gram ➜ gr _____

3. trot ➜ tr _____   8. plan ➜ pl _____

4. spot ➜ sp _____   9. sled ➜ sl _____

5. clam ➜ cl _____   10. drum ➜ dr _____

Switching Letters

Directions: Change the first letter of each given word to make a new word. Use your flip book to help you.

1. glow → _____ low

2. flap → _____ lap

3. fled → _____ led

4. grow → _____ row

5. clip → _____ lip

6. trip → _____ rip

7. slug → _____ lug

8. plow → _____ low

Talk

Directions: Use your flip book to help you fill in the missing letters in the conversations below.

1. When did you draw that?

   I ___ ___ ___ w that yesterday.

2. When did you fly on an airplane?

   I ___ ___ ___ w on an airplane last year.

3. Did you grow since last year?

   Yes, of course I ___ ___ ___ w.

4. Did you see the dancer spin?

   Yes, she looked so pretty as she ___ ___ ___ n.

Winter Words

Directions: Use the clues below and your flip book to help you finish each word in the snowflakes.

Winter Word Clues

1. Walk carefully on icy surfaces so you do not do this. This word can be found in the word *slipper*. You wear this under a thin skirt.

2. In the snow, you can ride on this down hills. This object has runners to help it slide. Dogs are sometimes used to pull these objects over ice.

3. This hot dish is a thick soup. Ingredients might contain carrots, beef, and potatoes.

4. This vehicle moves snow off of roads and parking lots. This vehicle has a large shovel on its front.

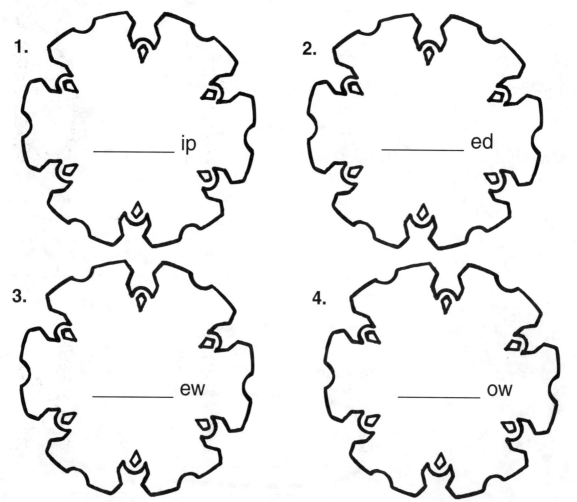

1. _____ ip

2. _____ ed

3. _____ ew

4. _____ ow

Ending Letter Blends Flip Book

Directions: Make a flip book for each student.

1. Copy pages 55–59.

2. Cut out the strips along the outside dashed lines.

3. Cut the boxes vertically, cutting only on the dashed lines. Make sure not to cut on the solid lines.

4. Stack the strips on top of each other and staple them together where the staple marks are indicated.

staple	staple	staple	staple
b	a	f	d

staple	staple	staple	staple
c	e	l	k

Ending Letter Blends Flip Book (cont.)

staple	staple	staple	staple
d	i	m	p

staple	staple	staple	staple
f	o	n	t

staple	staple	staple	staple
h	u	s	

Ending Letter Blends Flip Book (cont.)

staple	staple	staple	staple

l

staple	staple	staple	staple

m

staple	staple	staple	staple

n

Ending Letter Blends Flip Book (cont.)

staple	staple	staple	staple
p			

staple	staple	staple	staple
r			

staple	staple	staple	staple
s			

Ending Letter Blends Flip Book *(cont.)*

staple	staple	staple	staple
t			

staple	staple	staple	staple
v			

staple	staple	staple	staple
w			

Ending Letter Blends Word List

Listed below are some words that can be made using the Ending Letter Blends Flip Book.

raft	mask	bald	bent	camp	cast
lift	task	held	cent	damp	fast
sift	desk	weld	dent	lamp	last
loft	disk	mild	lent	ramp	mast
soft	risk	wild	rent	limp	past
	dusk	bold	sent	romp	best
help	husk	cold	tent	bump	nest
pulp	tusk	fold	vent	dump	pest
		hold	went	hump	rest
band	bank	mold	hint	lump	test
hand	dank	sold	lint	pump	vest
land	rank	told	mint		west
sand	sank		pint	talk	fist
wand	tank	halt	tint	walk	list
bend	link	malt	hunt	milk	mist
lend	pink	salt	punt	silk	host
mend	rink	belt	runt	folk	lost
send	sink	felt		bulk	most
bind	wink	melt	wasp	sulk	post
find	honk	welt	lisp		bust
mind	bunk	silt	wisp		dust
rind	dunk	tilt			must
wind	sunk	wilt			rust
bond		bolt			
fond		colt			
pond		molt			
fund		volt			

Activity Ideas for Teachers

The following activities can be used with the Ending Letter Blends Flip Book. Many of the activities have supporting materials. The page numbers where the materials can be found are provided.

=== **Pirate Letters** ===

Directions

1. Read the story *Pirate Letters* (below) aloud to the class.

2. Distribute copies of the handout on page 64.

3. Read the directions and questions on the handout aloud to the students. Have them work in groups, pairs, or individually to fill in the missing words in the answers using their flip books.

Pirate Letters

Once there was a band of pirates that liked to hunt for treasure at dusk. Whenever these pirates were near land, they would wait for the wind to blow, hop on their **raft**, and set up a tent in the sand before they began the task of looking for treasure.

They would sleep in their **tent** at **camp** in the wind, in cold, damp weather, and in the best weather. In fact, these pirates loved to rest in their tent so much that one day, these pirates sent a letter to their captain that said this:

*Please do not sulk, but we have felt for a long time that our days as pirates must halt. We do not like the task of raising up the mast of our ship. We wilt in the hot sun. We do not like the dank feeling in our cabin. We mind when we must dunk in the cold water to get clean. We do not like when we are lost at sea. We like to walk on **land**, feel the **sand** between our toes, put our treasure safely in the **bank**, and most of all—not worry that the boat we are on is going to sink.*

When the captain got the letter, he sat at his **desk** and began the task of writing a letter back.

I went to town as fast as I could, and I sold this ship for one cent. I don't want to be a pirate anymore, either! This was our last trip. Being a pirate is now in our past.

And with that, the pirate captain went to find his pirates. Together, they set up a camp near a freshwater **pond** and watched as their ship sailed away around a **bend**. As for their treasure . . . they had plenty already.

Answer Key: (Answers are also **bolded** throughout the story.)

1. raft	4. bank
2. tent, camp	5. land, sand, pond
3. desk	6. bend

Activity Ideas for Teachers *(cont.)*

Pirate Treasure

Directions

1. Before class, cut out the Pirate Treasure Cards on page 65.

2. Place the students into several groups.

3. Read *Pirate Letters* (page 61) aloud to the class. After reading the story, ask your students to imagine the answer to the question, "What was the pirates' treasure?"

4. Explain to the students that they are going to play a game to help them answer the question.

5. With their groups, have the students use their flip books to make some words found in the story.

6. When a group makes a word correctly, give that group a clue from the clue cards.

7. Once all the clues have been distributed, have the students share the clues with the other members of the class.

8. Have the class try to figure out the answer to the question by "unscrambling" the letters. You may choose to give the students an additional clue by telling them that the answer is two words.

Answer Key:

What was the pirates' treasure? *gold bars*

Blend at the End

Directions

1. Distribute copies of the handout on page 66.

2. Have your students work in pairs, groups, or individually.

3. Read each sentence aloud with your students.

4. Have them use their flip books to help them complete the missing words in the sentences.

Answer Key:

1. hand
2. raft
3. talk
4. bank

5. desk
6. rest
7. mint

Activity Ideas for Teachers *(cont.)*

Rotating Groups

Directions

1. Before class, label several lined pieces of paper with different ending blends (one ending blend per paper). Select from the following ending blends, depending on the number of groups you want: *-nd, -nt, -st, -sk, -ft, -ld, -lk, -lt, -mp, -nk.*

2. Place the papers in various parts of the room.

3. Assign a word ending to each student. Those students assigned to the same word ending will form a group. Give each group their assigned piece of paper from step 1.

4. Have the groups use their flip books to try to find words ending in their assigned letter blend. Have them write the words they find on the paper.

5. After several minutes, have the groups switch ending blends.

6. Have the groups use their flip books to find words that the group before them did not find. When a new word is found, have them add the word to the list.

7. Continue the activity until each group has had a chance to work with each letter blend, or until no words are left to be found. Use the Ending Letter Blends Word List on page 60 for possible answers.

8. Share the lists at the end of the activity.

For Sale

Directions

1. Distribute copies of the handout on page 67.

2. Have the students work individually, in pairs, or in groups.

3. Have the students use their flip books to help them complete the labels on the items that are for sale.

Answer Key:

soft tissues

cold soda

milk

orange juice with *pulp*

salt

bright *lamp*

pink lemonade

pint of ice cream

Pirate Letters

Directions: Use your flip book to help you answer the questions about the story.

1. How did the pirates get to land? The pirates used a r___ ___ ___ to get to land.

2. Where did the pirates sleep on land? The pirates slept in a t___ ___ ___ at c___ ___ ___.

3. Where did the pirate captain sit when he wrote his letter to the pirates? The pirate captain sat at a d___ ___ ___.

4. Where did the pirates want to put their money? The pirates wanted to put their money in a b___ ___ ___.

5. Where did the pirates want to live? The pirates wanted to live on l___ ___ ___, in the s___ ___ ___, and near a p___ ___ ___.

6. Where did the pirate ship go? The pirate ship went around a b___ ___ ___.

Pirate Treasure Cards

Directions: Cut along the dashed lines to separate the letter clues.

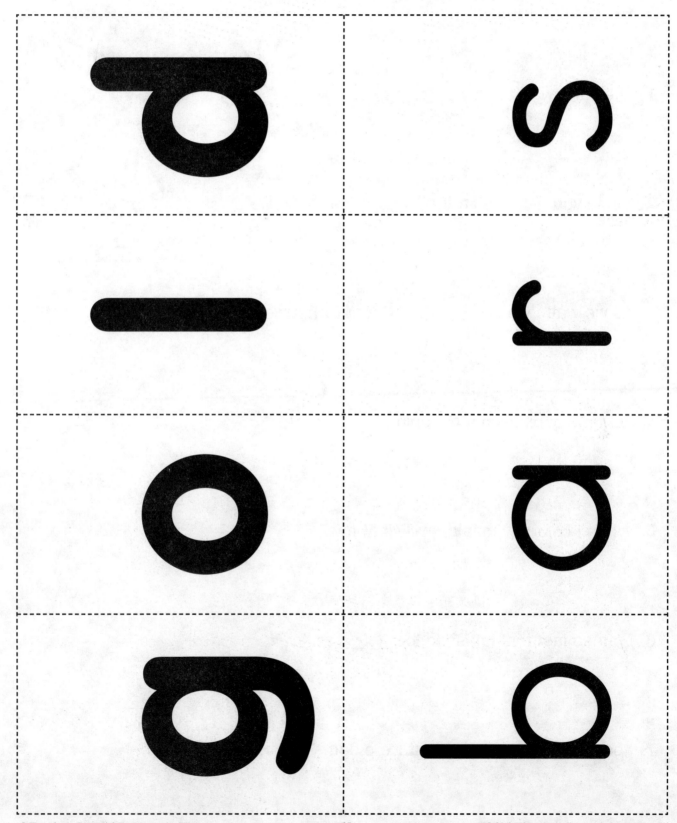

Blend at the End

Directions: Use your flip book to help you finish each sentence.

1. I held the wa**nd** in my ___ ___**nd**.

2. Could you help me li**ft** the ___ ___**ft** into the water?

3. As we wa**lk**, we can ___ ___**lk** about what we did during the day.

4. I put my pennies in a pi**nk** piggy ___ ___**nk**.

5. When I color my ma**sk**, I will sit at my ___ ___**sk**.

6. I ran so fa**st** that I needed to ___ ___**st**.

7. I bought a pi**nt** of ___ ___**nt** ice cream.

For Sale

Directions: Help the store label the items for sale. Use your flip book to help you.

___ ___ f ___ tissues

___ a ___ ___

c ___ ___ d soda

bright ___ ___ m ___

___ i ___ ___

p ___ ___ ___ lemonade

orange juice with ___ ___ l ___

___ i ___ ___ of ice cream

Letters C and G Flip Book

Directions: Make a very short Letters C and G Flip Book for each student.

1. Copy the letters *c* and *g* below for each of your students.

2. Cut out the boxes along the outside dashed lines.

3. Staple the boxes on top of each other where the staple marks are indicated.

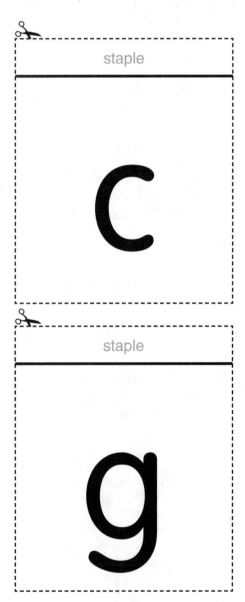

staple

c

staple

g

Activity Ideas for Teachers

The following activities can be used with the Letters C and G Flip Book. One of the activities has supporting materials. The page numbers where the materials can be found are provided.

Mysterious Letters

Directions

1. Explain to the students that the letters *c* and *g* are mysterious letters. These letters make more than one sound.

   - The letter *c* can sound like an *s*, as in the word *cell*. Or, it can sound like a *k*, like in the word *call*.

   - The letter *g* can sound like a *j*, as in the word *giraffe*. Or, it can sound like the *g* in the word *gate*.

2. Then explain that you are going to read aloud a list of words. The students must decide if each word contains the letter *c* or the letter *g*. The students should use their flip books to show you which letter they feel is used in each word.

3. One by one, read the words aloud, accenting the sound that you want the students to hear. (These sounds are in **bold**.) Look at the flip books that the students hold up to make sure they have identified the correct letter.

Read Aloud: **c**ame, **c**an, dan**c**e, prin**c**ess, **g**o, **g**ood, a**g**e, **g**reen, **c**ity, **c**ookie, **g**reat, pa**g**e, i**c**e, fa**c**e, fragile, **c**ity, **g**em

Missing Letters

Directions

1. Before class, cut out the flashcards provided on pages 70–72.

2. Have the students work in pairs, groups, or individually.

3. Explain to them that you will be holding up some flashcards. There will be a letter missing from each of the words. The students must decide whether the letter *c* or the letter *g* is missing from each word. When the students have decided which letter is missing, they should hold up their flip books for you to see.

4. Hold up the flashcards one at a time. Allow students time to figure out which letter is missing, and to show it to you.

Answer Key: (missing letters are in **bold**)

i**c**e, **g**erm, **c**ar, **c**ome, big, **c**an't, **g**et, fa**c**e, **g**ood, on**c**e, bag, a**c**e or a**g**e, **g**ave or **c**ave, **g**old or **c**old

Missing Letters

Directions: Cut out the flashcards along the dashed lines.

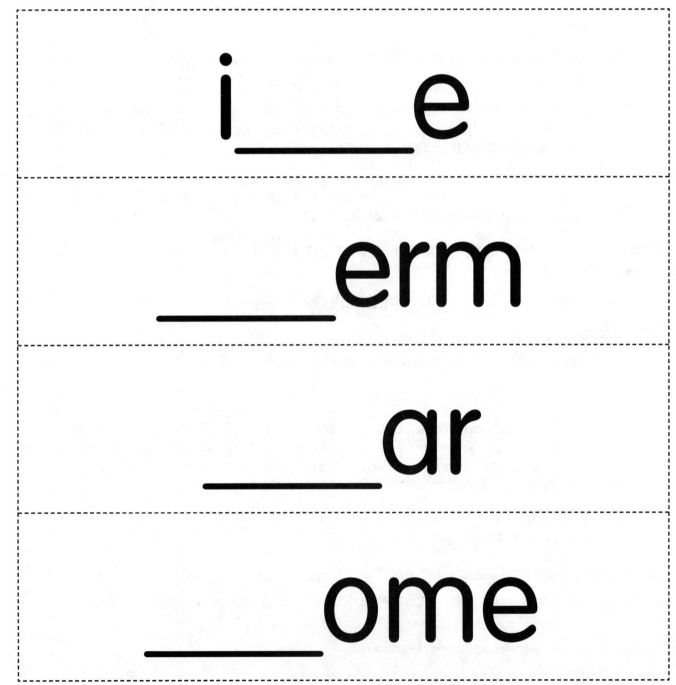

i___e

___erm

___ar

___ome

Missing Letters (cont.)

bi_____

_____an't

_____et

fa_____e

_____ood

Missing Letters *(cont.)*

on___e

ba___

a___e

___ave

___old

72

Double Vowels Flip Book

Directions: Make a flip book for each student.

1. Copy pages 73–78.

2. Cut out the strips along the outside dashed lines.

3. Cut the boxes vertically, cutting only on the dashed lines. Make sure not to cut on the solid lines.

4. Stack the strips on top of each other and staple them together where the staple marks are indicated.

staple	staple	staple
b	ai	d

staple	staple	staple
c	ea	f

Double Vowels Flip Book (cont.)

staple	staple	staple
d	ee	k

staple	staple	staple
f	oa	l

staple	staple	staple
g	oi	m

Double Vowels Flip Book *(cont.)*

staple	staple	staple
h	oo	n

staple	staple	staple
j	ou	p

staple	staple	staple
l		r

Double Vowels Flip Book (cont.)

staple	staple	staple
m		t

staple	staple	staple
n		

staple	staple	staple
p		

Double Vowels Flip Book (cont.)

staple	staple	staple
r		

staple	staple	staple
s		

staple	staple	staple
t		

Double Vowels Flip Book (cont.)

staple	staple	staple
W		

Double Vowels Word List

Listed below are some words that can be made using the Double Vowels Flip Book.

bail	gain	jail	mail	pail	rail	tail
bait	gait	laid	main	pain	rain	wail
fail	hail	lair	nail	pair	said	wait
fair	hair	maid	paid	raid	sail	

bead	dead	gear	jean	meal	peal	seam	weak
beak	deaf	head	lead	mean	pear	sear	wear
beam	deal	heal	leaf	meat	read	seat	
bean	dear	heap	leak	near	real	teal	
bear	fear	hear	lean	neat	rear	team	
beat	feat	heat	leap	peak	seal	tear	

beef	deep	feet	need	reed	seek	teen
beep	deer	heel	peek	reef	seem	weed
beet	feed	meek	peel	reel	seen	week
deed	feel	meet	peer	seed	seep	weep

boar	foal	load	moat	soak
boat	foam	loaf	road	soap
coal	goal	loan	roam	soar
coat	goat	moan	roar	toad

book	door	hood	look	moon	room	tool
boot	food	hoof	loom	nook	root	toot
cook	fool	hook	loop	noon	soon	wood
cool	foot	hoop	loot	pool	soot	woof
doom	good	hoot	mood	roof	took	wool

boil	coil	coin	foil	join	soil	toil

foul	loud	noun	pour	soul	soup	sour

Activity Ideas for Teachers

The following activities can be used with the Double Vowels Flip Book. All of the activities have supporting materials. The page numbers where the materials can be found are provided.

━━━━ Noisy Vowels ━━━━

Directions

1. Distribute copies of the handout on page 85.

2. Read each question aloud to your students.

3. Have your students work in groups, pairs, or individually to answer each question by making a word with a double vowel. Remind them that the words they are making are of sounds that people or animals would make.

4. Have the students show you the word in their flip books. If the word is correct, have them fill in the missing letters on their papers.

Answer Key:

1. wail
2. roar
3. goal
4. woof
5. hoot

━━━━ Signs ━━━━

Directions

1. Distribute copies of the handout on page 86.

2. Read aloud the different signs on the handout. As you are reading the signs aloud, say the word "blank" for each word that is incomplete.

3. Instruct your students to use their flip books to help them complete the words on the signs.

Answer Key:

1. hair
2. wait
3. feed, bear
4. door
5. wood
6. deer, road

━━━━ Double Vowels at the Beach ━━━━

Directions

1. Distribute copies of the handout on page 87.

2. Explain to the students that they will be using their flip books to help them make the words that describe the pictures of items on the beach.

Answer Key:

1. *rain* cloud
2. sun*beam*
3. *sailboat*
4. *deep* water
5. *book* to *read*
6. *pool*
7. *food* to eat

Activity Ideas for Teachers *(cont.)*

Unlock the Code

Directions

1. Distribute copies of the handout on page 88.
2. Explain to the students that one double-vowel combination will be used for all the words within a sentence. (One sentence will use all *ai*, another will use all *oa*, etc.)
3. Students should use their flip books to help them discover which double-vowel combination will work for all the words within a sentence.
4. Show the students the following example:

   The g ___ ___ l of the b ___ ___ t was to r ___ ___ m around the m ___ ___ t.

   Try a few double-vowel combinations to show the students what would not work. *Gool*, *geal*, and *geel* are not words. But the *oa* double-vowel combination works for all the incomplete words. "The *goal* of the *boat* was to *roam* around the *moat*." Show the students that the *oa* combination works in all the incomplete words in the sentence.
5. When the students are finished, read the completed sentences aloud to them.

Answer Key:

1. I *fear* the *mean bear* is *near* enough to smell my *bean* and *pear* salad.
2. I *feel* the *need* to *peek* at the *heel* of one of my *feet*.
3. The *toad* and the *goat* shared a *loaf* of bread on the *road*.
4. I like to *look* at the *moon* (12 hours from *noon*) from my *room* while eating some *good food*.
5. I *paid* for the *nail* and the *pail* so I would not be sent to *jail*, where I'd *wail*.

Close, but Not the Same

Directions

1. Distribute copies of the handout on page 89.
2. Explain to the students that the goal of the activity is to discover which double-letter vowels sound the same.
3. Model how the students should complete the handout. Say, "Well, the first word says *pair*. Let me look through my flip book to see what other vowel combination can make the same sound. The double vowel *oo* would make the word *poor*, but that sounds different than the word *pair*, so that is not the answer. If I put in the *ea* combination, I will get the word *pear*, which is a fruit. *Pear* sounds the same as *pair*, so I know that I have found the right answer."
4. Depending on the skill level of the students, you may want to complete the rest of the handout with them by examining different vowel combinations until the correct one is found, or you might ask the students to complete the rest of the answers as individuals, in pairs, or in groups.

Answer Key:

1. pair and pear
2. reel and real
3. weak and week
4. dear and deer
5. feat and feet
6. beat and beet
7. heal and heel
8. meat and meet

Activity Ideas for Teachers *(cont.)*

Bear Pairs

Directions

1. Distribute copies of the handout on page 90.

2. Have the students use their flip books to finish making the words located inside each of the bears.

3. Then have the students draw lines to match the words with the same middle letters.

Answer Key: Answers will vary. Use the Double Vowels Word List on page 79 for possible answers.

Balloons

Directions

1. Distribute copies of the handout on page 91.

2. Have the students use their flip books to finish the words that are located inside of the balloons.

3. Have the students practice reading the words that they have made.

4. Students may lightly color the balloons when they are finished.

Answer Key: Answers may include:

book, boot, cook, cool, doom, door, food, fool, foot, good, hood, hoof, hook, hoop, hoot, look, loom, loop, loot, mood, moon, nook, noon, pool, roof, room, soon, soot, took, tool, toot, wood, woof, wool

Double Vowels

Activity Ideas for Teachers *(cont.)*

=== **Beginning Letters** ===

Directions

1. Distribute copies of the handout on page 92.

2. Have the students use their flip books to finish the words that are next to the pictures.

3. Have students work in pairs or in groups to practice reading the words that they made.

Answer Key: Answers will vary. Answers may include:

coin, join

pear, tear, bear, dear, fear, hear, near, rear, sear, gear, wear

book, cook, look, nook, took, hook

pail, bail, fail, wail, hail, jail, sail, mail, nail, rail, tail

=== **Picture Pass** ===

Directions

1. Before class, cut out the pictures on pages 93–95.

2. During class, show the entire class each picture. Together with the class, figure out what each picture represents.

1. hair	5. seal	9. soil
2. moon	6. coin	10. pear
3. sour	7. boot	11. pool
4. loud	8. mail	12. jail

3. Break the class up into small groups. Give each group one picture.

4. Direct the students to use their flip books to make the word that describes the picture they were assigned. Have each group hold up their picture and word for you to see.

5. Tell the students to pass their picture to another group, and take a new picture. Repeat the process until each group has had a turn to make many of the words.

Activity Ideas for Teachers *(cont.)*

Clown Around

Directions

1. Distribute copies of the handout on page 96.

2. Have the students use their flip books to help them complete the words inside the balls that the clown is juggling.

3. Then place the students into pairs. Have them practice reading the words that they made.

Answer Key: Answers will vary. Use the Double Vowels Word List on page 79 for possible answers.

String of Pearls

Directions

1. Distribute copies of the handout on page 97.

2. Have the students use their flip books to help them complete the words inside the pearls.

3. Then place the students into pairs. Have them practice reading the words that they made.

Answer Key: Answers may include:

bead	feat	lean	rear
beak	gear	meal	seal
beam	head	mean	seam
bean	heal	meat	sear
bear	heap	near	seat
beat	hear	neat	teal
dead	heat	peak	team
deaf	jean	peal	tear
deal	lead	pear	weak
dear	leaf	read	wear
fear	leak	real	

Noisy Vowels

Directions: Use your flip book to help you make words that answer each question. Remember, each word is a noisy word!

1. What do unhappy babies do in the middle of the night?

   w ___ ___ l

2. What does a momma bear do to protect her cub?

   r ___ ___ r

3. What does a soccer coach like to yell out during a game?

   g ___ ___ l

4. What sound does a dog make?

   w ___ ___ f

5. What noise does an owl make?

   h ___ ___ t

Signs

Directions: Use your flip book to help you finish writing the words in the signs.

1.

Get your h ___ ___ r

cut here!

2.

W ___ ___ t to

be seated.

3.

Do not f ___ ___ d

the b ___ ___ r.

4.

Use the other

d ___ ___ r.

5.

Firew ___ ___ d

for sale.

6.

Watch for d ___ ___ r

on this r ___ ___ d.

86

Double Vowels at the Beach

Directions: Use your flip book to help you finish the words.

1. r ___ ___ n cloud

2. sunb ___ ___ m

3. s ___ ___ lb ___ ___ t

4. d ___ ___ p water

5. b ___ ___ k
   to r ___ ___ d

6. p ___ ___ l

7. f ___ ___ d
   to eat

87 *#8616 Flipping Over Making Words*

Unlock the Code

Directions: Use your flip book to help you figure out which vowel pair is missing from each sentence. Fill in the missing letters.

1. I f ___ ___ r the m ___ ___ n b ___ ___ r is n ___ ___ r enough to

   smell my b ___ ___ n and p ___ ___ r salad.

2. I f ___ ___ l the n ___ ___ d to p ___ ___ k at the h ___ ___ l of one

   of my f ___ ___ t.

3. The t ___ ___ d and the g ___ ___ t shared a l ___ ___ f of bread on

   the r ___ ___ d.

4. I like to l ___ ___ k at the m ___ ___ n (12 hours from n ___ ___ n)

   from my r ___ ___ m while eating some g ___ ___ d f ___ ___ d.

5. I p ___ ___ d for the n ___ ___ l and the p ___ ___ l so I would not be

   sent to j ___ ___ l, where I'd w ___ ___ l.

Close, but Not the Same

Directions: Use your flip book to help you find another set of vowels to complete each word pair. Each pair of words will sound the same, but the words will mean different things.

1.

pair and p ___ ___ r

5.

feat and f ___ ___ t

2.

reel and r ___ ___ l

6.

beat and b ___ ___ t

3.

weak and w ___ ___ k

7.

heal and h ___ ___ l

4.

dear and d ___ ___ r

8.

meat and m ___ ___ t

Bear Pairs

Directions: Use your flip book to help you finish the words inside the bears. Then draw lines to connect the bear pairs. Each pair of bears will have the same middle letters.

Balloons

Directions: Use your flip book to help you finish the words inside of the balloons.

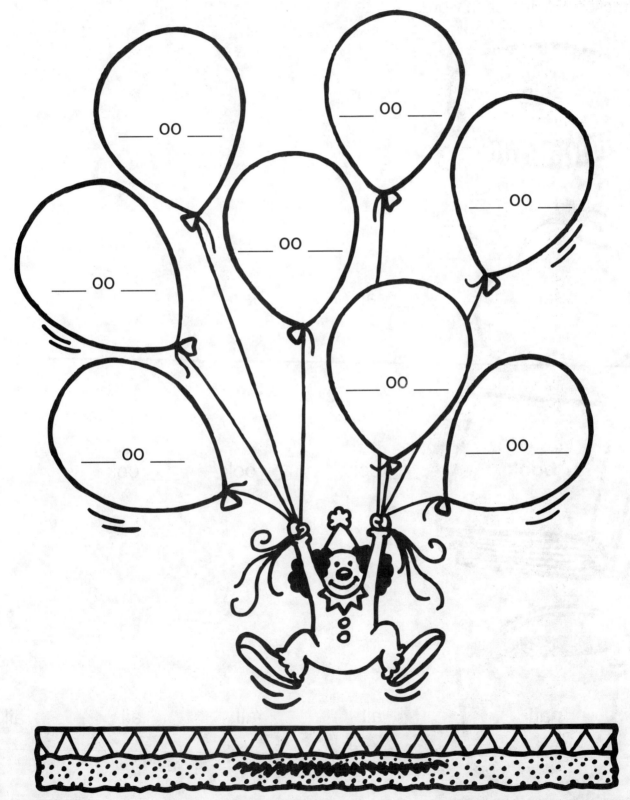

Beginning Letters

Directions: Use your flip book to help you finish the words located next to each picture. Change the first letter of each word in the pictures to make new words. Practice reading each word.

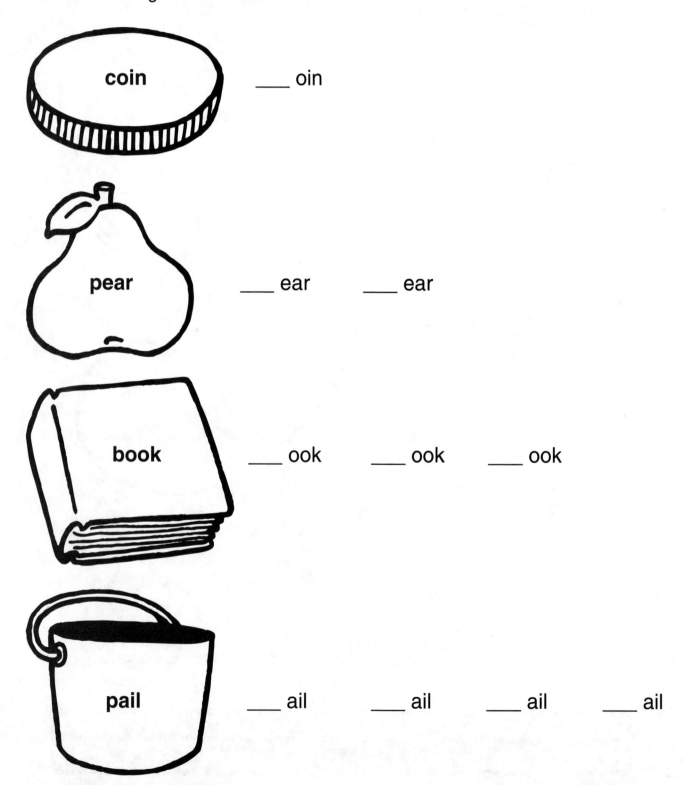

coin

___ oin

pear

___ ear   ___ ear

book

___ ook   ___ ook   ___ ook

pail

___ ail   ___ ail   ___ ail   ___ ail

Picture Pass

Directions: Cut out the picture cards along the dashed lines.

1.

2.

3.

4.

Picture Pass (cont.)

5.

6.

7.

8.

94

Picture Pass (cont.)

9.

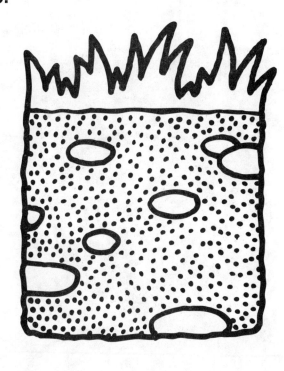

10.

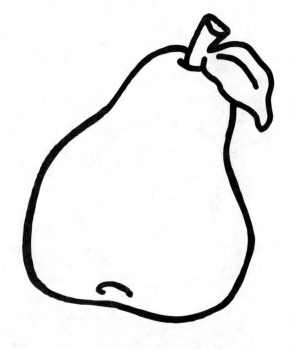

11.

12.

Clown Around

Directions: Help the clown juggle. Use your flip book to finish the words inside the balls.

___ ai ___

___ ou ___

___ ea ___

___ oo ___

___ oi ___

String of Pearls

Directions: Use your flip book to help you finish the words in each string of pearls.

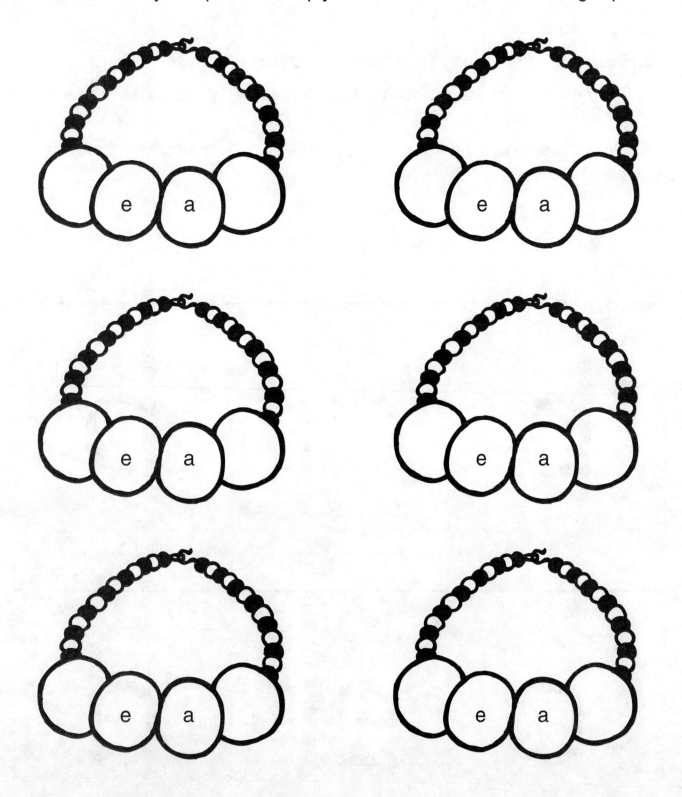

R-Controlled Vowels Flip Book

Directions: Make a flip book for each student.

1. Copy pages 98–102.

2. Cut out the strips along the outside dashed lines.

3. Cut the boxes vertically, cutting only on the dashed lines. Make sure not to cut on the solid lines.

4. Stack the strips on top of each other and staple them together where the staple marks are indicated.

staple	staple	staple
b	ar	b

staple	staple	staple
c	er	d

R-Controlled Vowels Flip Book (cont.)

staple	staple	staple

d ir e

staple	staple	staple

f or k

staple	staple	staple

g ur m

R-Controlled Vowels Flip Book (cont.)

staple	staple	staple
h		n

staple	staple	staple
l		p

staple	staple	staple
m		t

R-Controlled Vowels Flip Book *(cont.)*

staple	staple	staple
p		

staple	staple	staple
s		

staple	staple	staple
t		

R-Controlled Vowels Flip Book *(cont.)*

staple	staple	staple
V		

staple	staple	staple
W		

R-Controlled Vowels Word List

Listed below are some words that can be made using the R-Controlled Vowels Flip Book.

bare	care	dart	hare	lark	park	warm
bark	cart	fare	harm	mare	part	wart
barn	dare	farm	harp	mark	tarp	
card	dark	hard	lard	mart	tart	

fern	germ	herb	herd	here	perk	term	verb	were

bird	dirt	fire	firm	hire	tire	wire

bore	cork	fort	morn	sort	wore
born	corn	horn	pork	tore	work
cord	fork	lord	port	torn	worm
core	form	more	sore	word	worn

burn	burp	curb	cure	hurt	pure	sure	turn

Activity Ideas for Teachers

The following activities can be used with the R-Controlled Vowels Flip Book. Many of the activities have supporting materials. The page numbers where the materials can be found are provided.

═══ Finish It ═══

Directions

1. Distribute copies of the handout on page 106.

2. Instruct the students to use their flip books to help them finish the word sets on their handouts. Each word set can be made into three different words.

3. Complete the first set of words together. Show the students how they can use their flip books to make the words *harp*, *hard*, *hare*, or *harm* just by flipping the last column of their flip books.

4. Have the students work individually, in pairs, or in groups to complete the remaining sets of words.

Answer Key: Answers may include:

A. hard, hare, harm, harp

B. card, care, cart

C. word, wore, work, worm, worn

D. bare, care, dare, fare, hare, mare

E. bore, core, more, sore, tore, wore

F. farm, firm, form

G. were, wire, wore

═══ All Mixed Up ═══

Directions

1. Before class, cut out the strips of mixed-up letters on pages 107–108.

2. During class, hold up one strip at a time.

3. Have the students use their flip books to put the letters in the correct order so that a word is made. Have the students start with the vowel/r-combination, then arrange the other letters.

4. Have the students hold up the word they have made for you to see.

Answer Key:

1. bark	3. corn	5. dark	7. sure	9. hurt
2. bird	4. here	6. card	8. word	10. fire

═══ Look Alikes ═══

Directions

1. Distribute copies of the handout on page 109.

2. Have the students work individually, in pairs, or in groups to add R-controlled vowels to the blank spaces in each word to create different words. The students should use their flip books to help them.

Answer Key: Answers will vary. Use the R-Controlled Vowels Word List on page 103 for possible answers.

Activity Ideas for Teachers *(cont.)*

━━━━━━━━━━━━━━━━━━━ **Sentence Match** ━━━━━━━━━━━━━━━━━━━

Directions

1. Distribute copies of the handout on page 110.

2. Have the students work individually, in pairs, or in groups to add R-controlled vowels to the blank spaces in each word.

3. Have the students match the sentences to the pictures on the page.

Answer Key:

1. A *lark* is a kind of *bird*.

2. There is a *barn* on the *farm*.

3. There is a *worm* in the *dirt*.

━━━━━━━━━━━━━━━━━━━ **At the Farm** ━━━━━━━━━━━━━━━━━━━

Directions:

1. Distribute copies of the handout on page 111.
2. Using their flip books, have the students work individually, in pairs, or in groups to make words that have R-controlled vowels.
3. Have the students write the words inside the corrals.

Answer Key: Answers will vary. Use the R-Controlled Vowels Word List on page 103 for possible answers.

━━━━━━━━━━━━━━━━━━━ **One Flip** ━━━━━━━━━━━━━━━━━━━

Directions

1. Have students make the word *bare* with their flip books.

2. Then, have the students flip the last letter in order to create the word *bark*.

3. Explain to them that you will be calling out a few words. The students will need to flip only one letter (or column) in the word in order to make the new word. Have the students hold up their flip books to show you the words that they make.

4. After the words *bare* and *bark*, call out the following words: *dark*, *dare*, *mare*, *more*, *tore*, *tire*, *fire*, and *firm*.

Finish It

Directions: Finish the words that have been started. Use your flip book to help you. Each word can be finished at least three different ways.

A.

1. har _____

2. har _____

3. har _____

B.

1. car _____

2. car _____

3. car _____

C.

1. wor _____

2. wor _____

3. wor _____

D.

1. _____ are

2. _____ are

3. _____ are

E.

1. _____ ore

2. _____ ore

3. _____ ore

F.

1. f _____ m

2. f _____ m

3. f _____ m

G.

1. w _____ e

2. w _____ e

3. w _____ e

All Mixed Up

Directions: Cut out the strips of mixed-up letters along the dashed lines.

1.

ar | b | k

2.

d | b | ir

3.

n | or | c

4.

er | e | h

5.

k | d | ar

All Mixed Up *(cont.)*

6.		
d	c	ar
7.		
e	ur	s
8.		
w	d	or
9.		
ur	h	t
10.		
e	ir	f

Look Alikes

Directions: The first and the last letter look the same in each pair. Add center letters to make two different words. Use your flip book to help you.

1. p ___ ___ k   p ___ ___ k

2. t ___ ___ e   t ___ ___ e

3. t ___ ___ n   t ___ ___ n

4. f ___ ___ m   f ___ ___ m

5. w ___ ___ e   w ___ ___ e

6. w ___ ___ m   w ___ ___ m

Sentence Match

Directions: Complete the sentences by adding the missing letters to the words. Use your flip book to help you. Match the sentences to the pictures on the page.

1. A l ___ ___ k is a kind

of b ___ ___ d.

2. There is a b ___ ___ n

on the f ___ ___ m.

3. There is a w ___ ___ m

in the d ___ ___ t.

At the Farm

Directions: Help the farmer round up the R-controlled vowels. Use your flip book to help you make words that have R-controlled vowels. Write a word inside each corral.

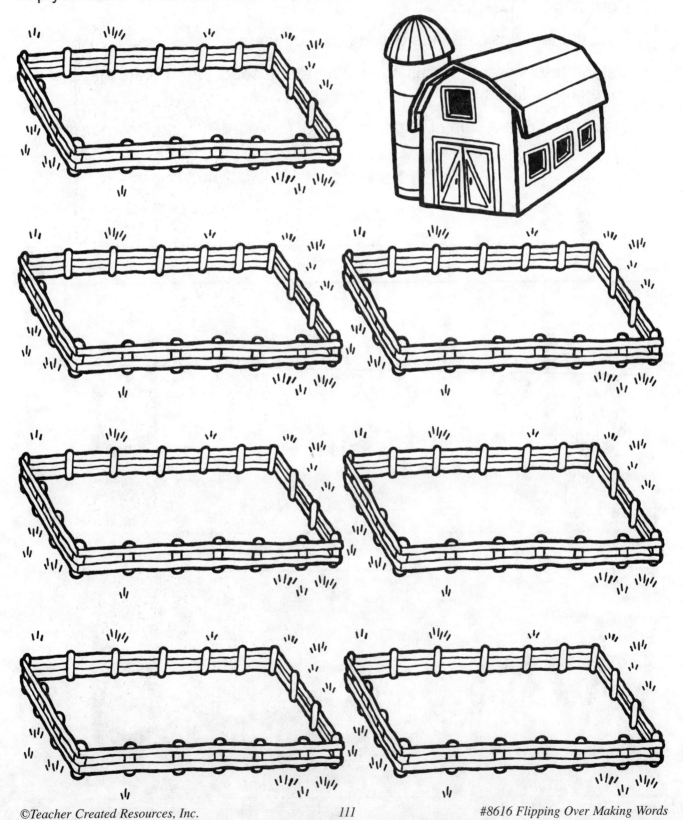

Beginning Digraphs Flip Book

Directions: Make a flip book for each student.

1. Copy pages 112–115.

2. Cut out the strips along the outside dashed lines.

3. Cut the boxes vertically, cutting only on the dashed lines. Make sure not to cut on the solid lines.

4. Stack the strips on top of each other and staple them together where the staple marks are indicated.

staple	staple	staple
ch	a	b

staple	staple	staple
wh	e	d

Beginning Digraphs Flip Book (cont.)

staple	staple	staple
sh	i	f

staple	staple	staple
th	o	g

staple	staple	staple
	u	m

Beginning Digraphs Flip Book (cont.)

staple	staple	staple
		n

staple	staple	staple
		p

staple	staple	staple
		re

114

Beginning Digraphs Flip Book (cont.)

staple	staple	staple
		se

staple	staple	staple
		t

staple	staple	staple
		te

Beginning Digraphs Word List

Listed below are some words that can be made using the Beginning Digraphs Flip Book.

chase	chin	chop	chose	chute
chat	chip	chore	chug	

wham	what	when	where	whim	whip	white	whose

share	shin	shop	shot
shed	ship	shore	shut

than	them	there	thin	thud
that	then	these	those	thug

Activity Ideas for Teachers

The following activities can be used with the Beginning Digraphs Flip Book. Many of the activities have supporting materials. The page numbers where the materials can be found are provided.

================================ **Ch-Wh-Sh** ================================

Directions

1. Divide the students into groups of three.

2. Distribute copies of the handout on page 119.

3. Have each student within a group complete one of the three incomplete words using the digraphs *ch*, *wh*, and *sh*. When a group has completed the three words correctly, read the question aloud to the students.

4. Have the students continue until they have completed all of the questions on the handout.

Answer Key:

1. *Where* did you *shop* for the shoes that you *chose*?
2. *What ship* did you see *chug* away?
3. *Whose chore* was it to *shut* the door?
4. *Where* in the *shed* did you hurt your *chin* (or *shin*)?
5. *Where* did you *chat* about the *shore*?

================================ **Picture Clues** ================================

Directions

1. Distribute copies of the handout on page 120.

2. Have the students use their flip books to help them make the words that describe the pictures.

Answer Key:

1. chin
2. ship
3. shop
4. shore
5. shed
6. what (or when)

================================ **Choo-Choo Train** ================================

Directions

1. Distribute copies of the handout on page 121.
2. Have the students work individually, in groups, or in pairs to complete the handout.
3. Instruct the students to use their flip books to make words that start with the *ch* digraph. As the students make their words, have them write the words on their handouts on the train cars.

Answer Key: Answers will include:

chase, chat, chin, chip, chop, chore, chose, chug, chute

Activity Ideas for Teachers *(cont.)*

===== **Ahoy!** =====

Directions

1. Distribute copies of the handout on page 122.

2. Instruct the students to use their flip books to help them complete the signs on and near the ship with words starting with *sh*. You may want to help the students to read the incomplete signs before they begin working.

3. This activity can be completed individually, in groups, or in pairs.

Answer Key:

Ocean Ship, The Ship's Shop, Welcome to the Shore, Share the Ocean, Keep this door shut

===== **Think!** =====

Directions

1. Distribute copies of the handout on page 123.

2. Using their flip books, have the students work individually, in pairs, or in groups to complete the handout.

3. Instruct the students to make words beginning with *th* and to write the words that they make inside each light bulb.

Answer Key: Answers may include:

than, that, them, then, there, these, thin, those, thud, thug

===== **Listen, Flip, and Lift** =====

Directions

1. Direct the students to use only the first column of their flip books. (You might want to have the students separate the first column of the flip books from the other columns, or you might want to make a mini flip book for each student with just the one section that they will need. Students will only need the *ch*, *sh*, and *wh* beginning digraphs for this activity.)

2. Instruct the students to *listen* to the words that you say, *flip* to the beginning digraph that you are using, and then *lift* the flip book up for you to see.

3. Read aloud the list of words provided, or use similar words. As you read each word, check to see that the students are holding up the correct beginning digraph.

Read Aloud Word List:

1. **wh**isper
2. **sh**oulder
3. **wh**ale
4. **sh**iver
5. **ch**ild
6. **ch**icken
7. **wh**eel
8. **sh**allow
9. **ch**ange
10. **wh**ile

Ch-Wh-Sh

Directions: Each question is missing one *ch*, one *wh*, and one *sh* beginning digraph. Have each person in your group use a flip book to make one of the missing words. Then show the words to your teacher.

1. _____ere did you _____op for the shoes that you _____ose?

2. _____at _____ip did you see _____ug away?

3. _____ose _____ore was it to _____ut the door?

4. _____ere in the _____ed did you hurt your _____in?

5. _____ere did you _____at about the _____ore?

Picture Clues

Directions: Use your flip book to help you make words that describe the pictures.

1. ____ ____ ____ ____

2. ____ ____ ____ ____

3. ____ ____ ____ ____

4. ____ ____ ____ ____ ____

5. ____ ____ ____ ____

6. ____ ____ ____ ____

Choo-Choo Train

Directions: Help the conductor load the train cars. Use your flip books to make words starting with *ch* and write them inside the train cars.

Ahoy!

Directions: Help the painter finish labeling the signs. Use your flip book to help you make the incomplete *sh* words on the signs.

Ocean

_____ _____ _____ p

Welcome to the

_____ _____ _____ _____ re

_____ _____ _____ re

the Ocean

The Ship's

_____ _____ _____ p

Keep this door

_____ _____ _____ t

Think!

Directions: Using your flip books, see if you can make words that start with *th*. Write the words in the light bulbs.

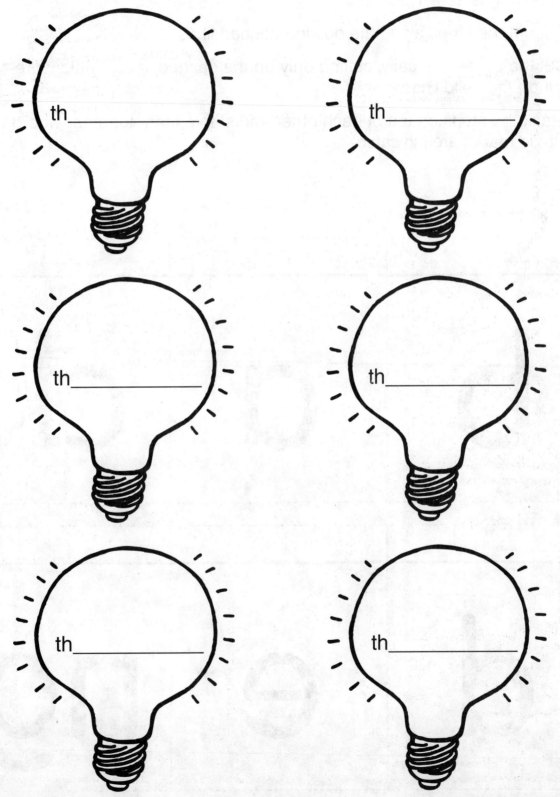

Ending Digraphs Flip Book

Directions: Make a flip book for each student.

1. Copy pages 124–127.

2. Cut out the strips along the outside dashed lines.

3. Cut the boxes vertically, cutting only on the dashed lines. Make sure not to cut on the solid lines.

4. Stack the strips on top of each other and staple them together where the staple marks are indicated.

staple	staple	staple
b	a	ck

staple	staple	staple
d	e	ng

Ending Digraphs Flip Book (cont.)

staple	staple	staple
f	i	sh

staple	staple	staple
h	o	th

staple	staple	staple
k	u	

Ending Digraphs Flip Book *(cont.)*

staple	staple	staple
m		

staple	staple	staple
p		

staple	staple	staple
r		

Ending Digraphs Flip Book *(cont.)*

staple	staple	staple
S		

staple	staple	staple
W		

Ending Digraphs Word List

Listed below are some words that can be made using the Ending Digraphs Flip Book.

back	dock	peck	rack	sick
buck	kick	pick	rock	sock
deck	pack	puck	sack	wick

bang	hung	ring	song
fang	king	sang	sung
hang	rang	sing	wing

bash	dish	mash	push	sash
bush	fish	mesh	rash	wash
dash	hush	mush	rush	wish

bath	math	path
both	moth	with

Activity Ideas for Teachers

The following activities can be used with the Ending Digraphs Flip Book. All of the activities have supporting materials. The page numbers where the materials can be found are provided.

Wishing Stars

Directions

1. Distribute copies of the handout on page 131.
2. Using their flip books, have the students work individually, in pairs, or in groups to make words ending with *sh*.
3. Have the students write the *sh* words that they make inside the wishing stars.
4. Then help the students write a wish on the bottom of the page or have the students draw a picture of their wish on the back.

Answer Key: Answers may include:

bash, bush, dash, hush, mash, mesh, mush, push, rash, rush, wash, wish

Name the Horses

Directions

1. Distribute copies of the handout on page 132.
2. Have the students work individually, in pairs, or in groups in order to give names to the horses on the page.
3. Instruct the students to make words that end with *ck*, *ng*, *th*, and *sh*. Students should write the words that they make on the horses. These words will be the horses' names.

Note: Explain to students that the "names" they will come up with might not sound like typical names. Remind students that names are capitalized.

Answer Key: Answers may include:

Back, Buck, Deck, Dock, Kick, Pack, Peck, Pick, Puck, Rack, Rock, Sack, Sick, Sock, Wick

Bang, Fang, Hang, Hung, King, Rang, Ring, Sang, Sing, Song, Sung, Wing

Bash, Bush, Dash, Dish, Fish, Hush, Mash, Mesh, Mush, Push, Rash, Rush, Sash, Wash, Wish

Bath, Both, Math, Moth, Path, With

A Busy Day

Directions

1. Distribute copies of the handout on page 133.
2. Have the students work individually, in pairs, or in groups to finish the poem by making words that rhyme with the words that are in **bold** letters.
3. Have the students write the words on their handouts.
4. Together with the class, read the poems aloud.
5. Have the students draw pictures that relate to the poems in the space provided.

Answer Key: Answers will vary. Possible poem:

On my **back** I put a **pack**,
On the **dock** I put a **rock**,
On a **king** I put a **ring**,
On a **dish** I put a **fish**,
On the **rack** I hung a **sack**,
"What a busy day," I did say.

Activity Ideas for Teachers *(cont.)*

Rhyming Cards

Directions

1. Before class, cut out the Rhyming Cards on pages 134–135.

2. During class, hold up a rhyming card. Have the students use their flip books to make the same word that you are holding up.

3. Then have the students make a word that rhymes with the word on the card. Have the students hold up the new word that they made so that you can see it.

   (This activity can be completed individually, in pairs, or in groups.)

Answer Key:

back: pack, rack, sack

rang: bang, fang, hang, sang

math: bath, path

wish: dish, fish

kick: pick, sick, wick

sing: king, ring, wing

Royal Rings

Directions

1. Distribute copies of the handout on page 136.
2. Using their flip books, have the students work individually, in pairs, or in groups to make words ending with *ng*.
3. Have the students write the *ng* words that they make inside the rings.

Answer Key: Answers may include:

bang, fang, hang, hung, king, rang, ring, sang, sing, song, sung, wing

Simply Rhymes

Directions

1. Instruct the students to work individually, in pairs, or in groups.

2. Call out a word from the Ending Digraphs Word List on page 128.

3. Have the students use their flip books to make the word that you say.

4. Then have them make a word that rhymes with the word that you say.

Example: Say the word *math*. The students should use their flip books to make the word *m-a-th*. Then the students could make the rhyming word *p-a-th* or *b-a-th*.

Wishing Stars

Directions: Write a word that ends with *sh* in each of the wishing stars. Use your flip book to help you. Then make a wish!

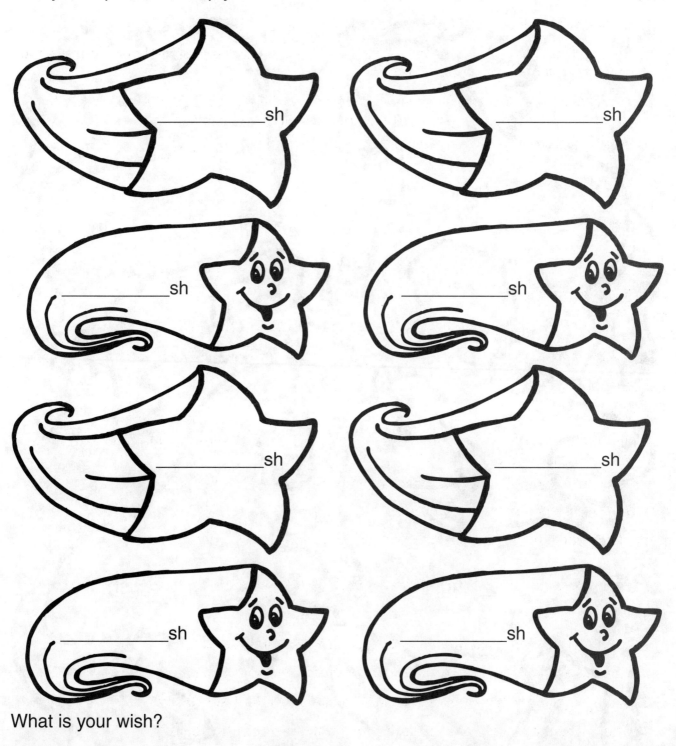

_____sh

_____sh

_____sh

_____sh

_____sh

_____sh

_____sh

_____sh

What is your wish?

_____

Name the Horses

Directions: Each horse needs a name. Help give the horses names by adding beginning letters to each name. Use your flip book to help you.

___ ___ ck

___ ___ th

___ ___ ng

___ ___ sh

A Busy Day

Directions: Finish the poem by adding in words that rhyme with the words that are in **bold**. Then draw a picture in the space below about something in the poem.

On my ___ ___ ___ ___ I put a **pack**,

On the **dock** I put a ___ ___ ___ ___,

On a **king** I put a ___ ___ ___ ___,

On a **dish** I put a ___ ___ ___ ___,

On the ___ ___ ___ ___ I hung a **sack**,

"What a busy day," I did say.

Rhyming Cards

Directions: Cut out the Rhyming Cards along the dashed lines.

b	a	ck
r	a	ng
m	a	th

Rhyming Cards (cont.)

w	i	sh
k	i	ck
s	i	ng

Royal Rings

Directions: Write a word that ends with *ng* inside each ring. Use your flip book to help you.

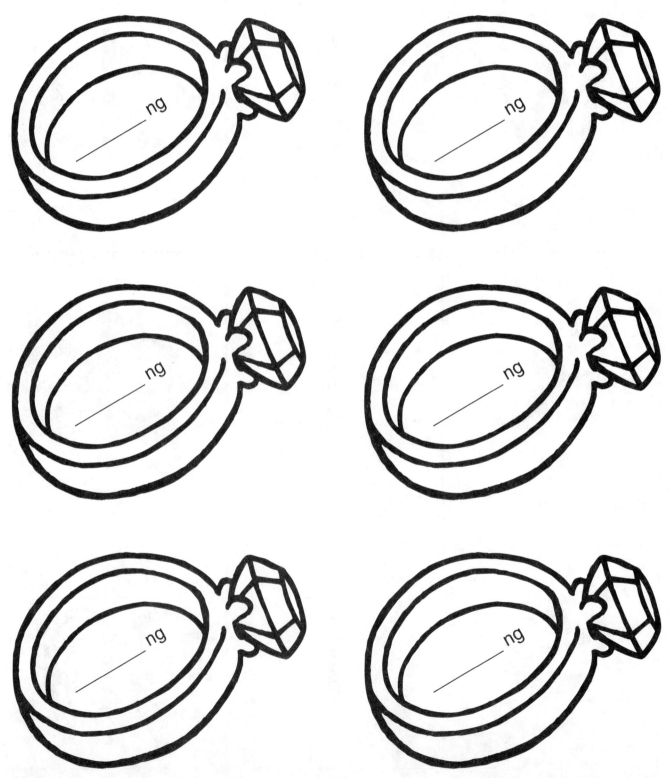

136

Silent H Flip Book

Directions: Make a flip book for each student.

1. Copy pages 137–141.

2. Cut out the strips along the outside dashed lines.

3. Cut the boxes vertically, cutting only on the dashed lines. Make sure not to cut on the solid lines.

4. Stack the strips on top of each other and staple them together where the staple marks are indicated.

staple	staple	staple
w	h	ale

staple	staple	staple
		at

Silent H Flip Book (cont.)

staple	staple	staple
		eat

staple	staple	staple
		eel

staple	staple	staple
		en

Silent H Flip Book *(cont.)*

staple	staple	staple
		ere

staple	staple	staple
		ich

staple	staple	staple
		irl

Silent H Flip Book (cont.)

staple	staple	staple
		ite

staple	staple	staple
		o

staple	staple	staple
		ole

Silent H Flip Book *(cont.)*

staple	staple	staple
		y

Silent H Word List

Listed below are some words that can be made using the Silent H Flip Book. **Note:** Although the words in *italics* can be made with the flip book, the *h* is not silent.

whale	wheat	when	which	white	*who*
what	wheel	where	whirl	*whole*	why

Activity Ideas for Teachers

The following activities can be used with the Silent H Flip Book. Many of the activities have supporting materials. The page numbers where the materials can be found are provided.

Question Words

Directions

1. Distribute copies of the handout on page 144.

2. Have the students use their flip books to help them identify and write question words.

3. Then place the students into pairs. Have them practice reading the words that they made.

Answer Key:
who, what, where, when, why, which

Silent H Bingo

Directions

1. Distribute copies of the blank Silent H Bingo board on page 145 along with small pieces of colored paper.

2. Instruct the students to use their flip books to help them make nine words that have a silent *h* in them. Have them write each word they make in a separate square anywhere on the Bingo board.

3. Tell the students that you will be calling out words. If the students have the word that you call out on their Bingo boards, they should place a piece of paper over that word space. When the students have covered three words in a row, they should call out, "Bingo!" (This may be the first time some of the students have played Bingo. You may want to walk around the room and help the students, or have students work in pairs or in groups to play with the different Bingo boards that they made.)

4. Using the Silent H Word List above, randomly call out words until the first student calls out "Bingo!"

5. Have the students remove the pieces of colored paper and play again. You may choose to play variations of Bingo, such as "black-out," where students cannot call out "Bingo!" until they have covered their entire board.

Activity Ideas for Teachers *(cont.)*

=== **Whale Tails** ===

Directions

1. Distribute copies of the handout on page 146.

2. Have the students use their flip books to help them complete the words inside the whale tails.

3. Then place the students into pairs. Have them practice reading the words that they made.

Answer Key: Answers may include:

whale, what, wheat, wheel, when, where, which, whirl, white, whole, who, why

=== **Who Knows?** ===

Directions

1. Have the students work individually, in pairs, or in groups to answer the questions listed below.

2. Read the questions aloud to the students and have the students use their flip books to make the correct answers. Students can hold up their flip books for you to see the answers.

Who Knows? Questions and Answers:

Who knows what the largest mammal in the sea is called? *whale*

Who knows what flour is often made from? *wheat*

Who knows what is round and helps things move? *wheel*

Who knows what color snow is? *white*

Who knows what two halves equal? *whole*

Question Words

Directions: Use your flip book to help you make words that are used at the beginning of questions.

Silent H

Silent H Bingo

Whale Tails

Directions: Write a word that begins with a *wh* inside each whale tail. Use your flip book to help you.

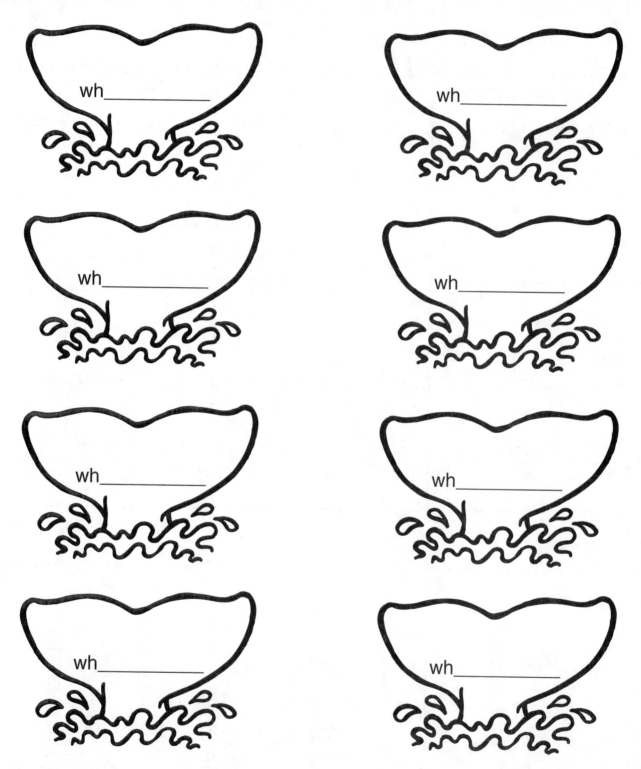

Silent B Flip Book

Directions: Make a flip book for each student.

1. Copy pages 147–149.

2. Cut out the strips along the outside dashed lines.

3. Cut the boxes vertically, cutting only on the dashed lines. Make sure not to cut on the solid lines.

4. Stack the strips on top of each other and staple them together where the staple marks are indicated.

staple	staple	staple
c	am	b

staple	staple	staple
cl	e	bt

Silent B Flip Book (cont.)

staple	staple	staple
cr im		

staple	staple	staple
d om		

staple	staple	staple
l ou		

Silent B Flip Book (cont.)

staple	staple	staple

th um

Silent B Word List

Listed below are some words that can be made using the Silent B Flip Book.

climb	crumb	limb	debt
comb	lamb	thumb	doubt

Activity Ideas for Teachers

The following activities can be used with the Silent B Flip Book. All of the activities have supporting materials. The page numbers where the materials can be found are provided.

Thumbs Up

Directions

1. Distribute copies of the handout on page 152.

2. Have the students work in pairs, groups, or individually to write words that have a silent *b* inside the pictures of a "thumbs up." The students should use their flip books to help them.

3. When the students are finished, check their answers. Give them a real "thumbs up" for doing a good job!

4. Place the students in pairs and have them practice reading the words that they made to each other.

Answer Key: Answers may include:

climb, comb, crumb, lamb, limb, thumb, debt, doubt

Activity Ideas for Teachers *(cont.)*

═══════════════════════ **Finish the Sentence** ═══════════════════════

Directions

1. Place the students in pairs, groups, or have them work individually. Distribute copies of the handout on page 153 accordingly.

2. Read the sentences aloud.

3. Have the students use their flip books to fill in the missing word in each sentence. Each missing word has a silent *b*.

Answer Key:

1. debt   5. doubt

2. climb   6. lamb

3. crumb   7. limb

4. comb   8. thumb

═══════════════════════ **Word Scramble** ═══════════════════════

Directions

1. Distribute copies of the handout on page 154.

2. Have the students use their flip books to help them unscramble the words on the page. Students can use the pictures as clues as well.

3. Once the students have unscrambled the words, have them draw lines to connect the words to the matching pictures on the page.

Answer Key:

1. comb

2. lamb

3. thumb

4. climb

5. crumb

6. doubt

Thumbs Up

Directions: Use your flip book to make words that have a silent *b*. Write your words inside the "thumbs up" pictures below.

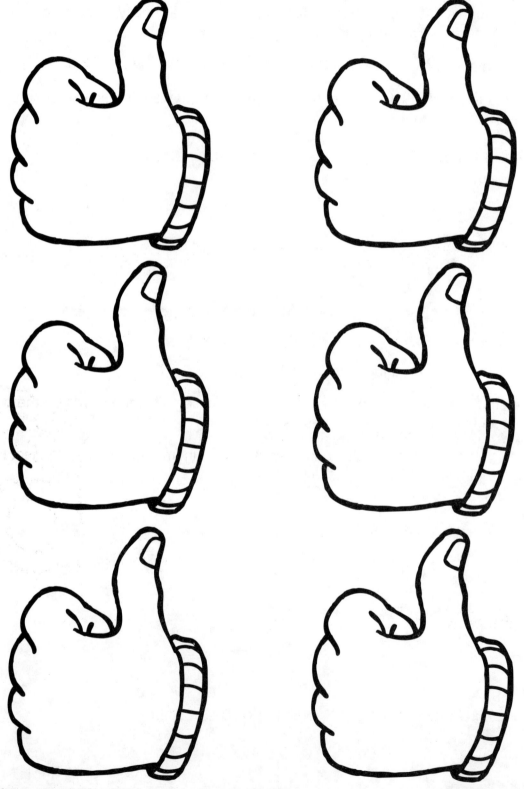

Finish the Sentence

Directions: Use your flip book to help you complete the sentences with words that have a silent *b*.

1. I am in _____, since I owe my brother five dollars.

2. The hiker tried to _____ the mountain.

3. When eating crackers in a fancy room, try not to drop a _____.

4. To get the knots out of my hair, I use a _____.

5. If I am not sure of something, I am in _____.

6. A baby sheep is called a _____.

7. During the heavy rain, a _____ fell off of an old tree.

8. When my daughter was young, she used to suck her _____.

Word Scramble

Directions: Use your flip book to help you unscramble the words below. Then match the words to the pictures. Each word has a silent *b*.

1. bmco ____ ____ ____ ____

2. malb ____ ____ ____ ____

3. tmbuh ____ ____ ____ ____ ____

4. cblim ____ ____ ____ ____ ____

5. cbrmu ____ ____ ____ ____ ____

6. uodbt ____ ____ ____ ____ ____

Silent L Flip Book

Directions: Make a flip book for each student.

1. Copy pages 155–157.

2. Cut out the strips along the outside dashed lines.

3. Cut the boxes vertically, cutting only on the dashed lines. Make sure not to cut on the solid lines.

4. Stack the strips on top of each other and staple them together where the staple marks are indicated.

staple	staple	staple
c	a	lk

staple	staple	staple
ch	ou	lf

Silent L Flip Book (cont.)

staple	staple	staple
h		ld

staple	staple	staple
sh		

staple	staple	staple
t		

Silent L Flip Book *(cont.)*

staple	staple	staple
W		

Silent L Word List

Listed below are some words that can be made using the Silent L Flip Book.

calf	could	talk	would
chalk	half	walk	should

Activity Ideas for Teachers

The following activities can be used with the Silent L Flip Book. All of the activities have supporting materials. The page numbers where the materials can be found are provided.

Lollipops

Directions

1. Distribute copies of the handout on page 160.

2. Have the students use their flip books to help them make words that have a silent *l*.

3. Have the students write their words inside of the lollipops.

4. Place the students in pairs or in small groups. Have them practice reading the words that they made to each other.

Answer Key: Answers will vary. See the Silent L Word List above for possible answers.

Activity Ideas for Teachers *(cont.)*

Palm Reading

Directions

1. Distribute copies of the handout on page 161.

2. Have the students use their flip books to help them finish making the words inside of the hands.

3. Then have them draw lines to connect the rhyming words.

4. Place the students in pairs. Have them practice reading the words on the page.

Answer Key:

talk, walk

could, would

calf, half

Palm Tree

Directions

1. Distribute copies of the handout on page 162.

2. Working independently, have the students use their flip books to help them finish making the words inside of the palm tree.

3. Then place the students in small groups. Have them practice reading the words on the page.

Answer Key: Answers may include:

calf

chalk

could

half

talk

walk

would

should

Lollipops

Directions: Use your flip books to help you make words that have a silent *l*. Write the words inside the lollipops.

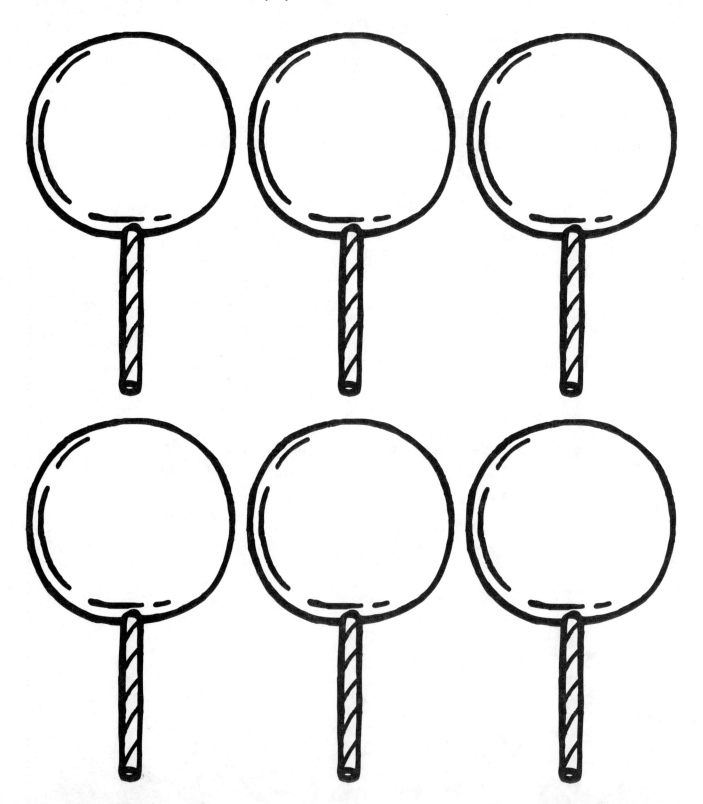

Palm Reading

Directions: Use your flip books to help you finish the words in the hands. Draw lines to match the words that rhyme.

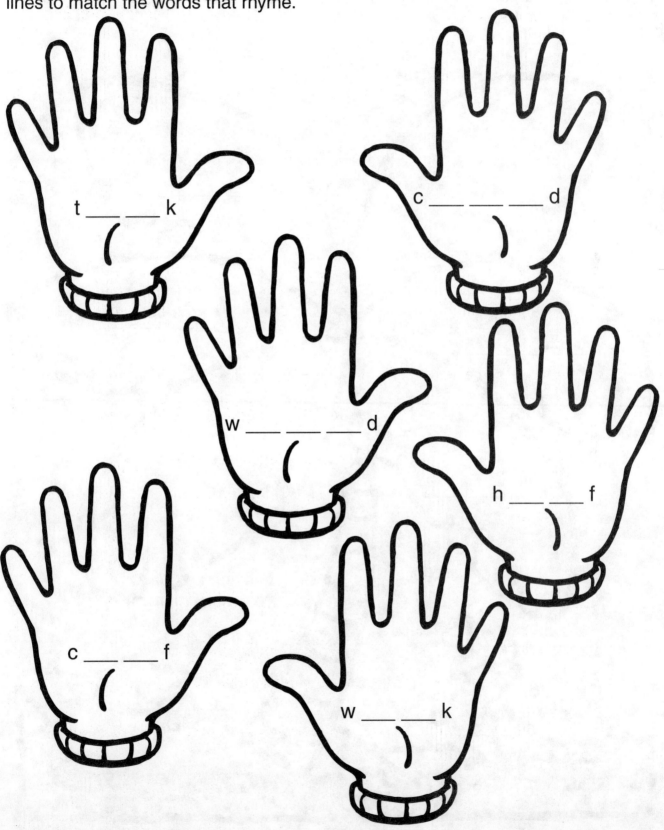

Palm Tree

Directions: The palm tree is missing some letters. Use your flip books to help you finish the words.

Common Endings Flip Book

Directions: Make a flip book for each student.

1. Copy pages 163–166.

2. Cut out the strips along the outside dashed lines.

3. Cut the boxes vertically, cutting only on the dashed lines. Make sure not to cut on the solid lines.

4. Stack the strips on top of each other and staple them together where the staple marks are indicated.

staple	staple
ask	s

staple	staple
call	ed

Common Endings Flip Book *(cont.)*

staple	staple
go	ing

staple	staple
help	

staple	staple
jump	

Common Endings Flip Book *(cont.)*

staple	staple
know	

staple	staple
look	

staple	staple
see	

Common Endings Flip Book *(cont.)*

staple	staple
think	

Common Endings Word List

Listed below are some words that can be made using the Common Endings Flip Book.

asks asked asking	calls called calling	going	helps helped helping
jumps jumped jumping	knows knowing	looks looked looking	sees seeing	thinks thinking

Activity Ideas for Teachers

The following activities can be used with the Common Endings Flip Book. All of the activities have supporting materials. The page numbers where the materials can be found are provided.

Ice Cream Scoops

Directions

1. Distribute copies of the handout on page 169.

2. Have the students use their flip books to help them finish making the words inside the ice cream scoops.

3. Place the students in pairs. Have them practice reading the words on the page.

Answer Key:

Triple Scoops: asks, asked, asking; jumps, jumped, jumping; looks, looked, looking

Double scoops: helps, helped, or helping; sees, seeing

Single Scoop: going

Snakes

Directions

1. Distribute copies of the handout on page 170.

2. Have the students use their flip books to help them make words that can end with the letter *s*. Have the students write those words inside the snakes.

3. Place the students in pairs. Have them practice reading the words on the page.

Answer Key:

asks, calls, jumps, knows, looks, sees, thinks, helps

Activity Ideas for Teachers *(cont.)*

Decisions

Directions

1. Distribute copies of the handout on page 171.

2. Read the story aloud to the students, with the missing words.

3. Place students into groups, pairs, or have them work individually.

4. Have the students use their flip books to help make words that will complete the story.

Answer Key:

"Grandma <u>called</u> on the phone," Mom said. "She <u>asked</u> what you wanted for your birthday."

"I want to go on a trip," the little girl said. She was so happy. She <u>jumped</u> up and down.

"Where do you want to go?" Grandma <u>asked</u> later that day.

"I don't know," the little girl said.

Grandma sent the little girl pictures of different places. The little girl <u>looked</u> through all of the pictures.

"The pictures <u>helped</u> me decide where I want to go," the little girl said. "I want to go to the Smoky Mountains."

Now Grandma <u>jumped</u> up and down. She was happy, too.

Singing Bird

Directions

1. Distribute copies of the handout on page 172.

2. Have the students use their flip books to help them make words that end in *ing*. Have the students write those words inside of the music notes.

3. Place the students in pairs. Have them practice reading (or singing!) the words on the page.

Answer Key: Answers may include:

asking, calling, going, knowing, looking, seeing, helping, thinking

Ice Cream Scoops

Directions: Finish making the words in the ice cream scoops by adding ending letters to the words. Use your flip book to help you.

ask _____

ask _____

ask _____

jump _____

jump _____

jump _____

look _____

look _____

look _____

help _____

help _____

see _____

see _____

go _____

Snakes

Directions: Use your flip book to help you make eight words that can end with the letter *s*.

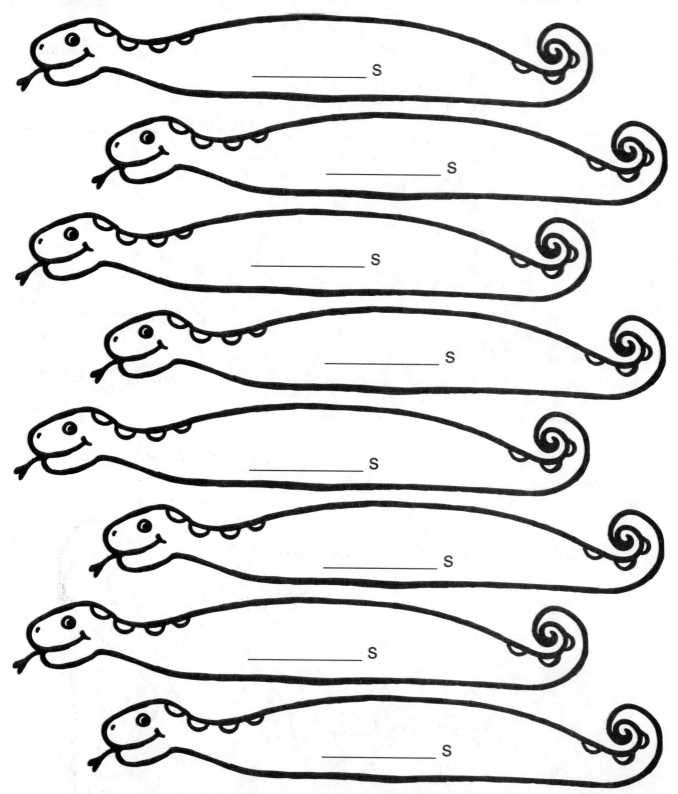

Decisions

Directions: Use your flip book to help you make words that will complete the missing words in the story.

"Grandma _____ed on the phone," Mom said. "She _____ed what you wanted for your birthday."

"I want to go on a trip," the little girl said. She was so happy. She _____ed up and down.

"Where do you want to go?" Grandma _____ed later that day.

"I don't know," the little girl said.

Grandma sent the little girl pictures of different places. The little girl _____ed through all of the pictures.

"The pictures _____ed me decide where I want to go," the little girl said. "I want to go to the Smoky Mountains."

Now Grandma _____ed up and down! She was happy, too.

Singing Bird

Directions: This little bird likes to sing words that end with the letters *ing*. Use your flip book to help you fill in the big music notes with words for the bird to sing. One music note was filled in for you.

jumping

Make Your Own Flip Book
Instruction Sheet

You can design your own flip books in order to help your students:
- learn new skills
- practice spelling words
- practice vocabulary words
- examine parts of speech or other grammar rules
- practice writing
- review word families and other reading skills

The possibilities are endless!

To make your own flip book:

First figure out what part of the words you want to focus on:
- beginning, middle, or ending sounds
- silent letters
- letter blends
- rhyming sounds
- syllable breaks
- vowel sounds
- prefixes/suffixes

Second, make your word list.
- Flip books work best when the words in the book are similar in some way.

Third, divide up your words into sections.
- Templates have been provided for two-, three-, and four-section flip books (see pages 174–176).

Fourth, place the word sections into the flip book templates.

Finally, make a flip book for each of your students.
1. Reproduce enough copies for each student.
2. Cut out the strips along the outside dashed lines.
3. Cut the boxes vertically, cutting only on the dashed lines. Make sure not to cut on the solid lines.
4. Stack the strips on top of each other and staple them together where the staple marks are indicated.

Two-Section
Flip Book Template

staple	staple

staple	staple

staple	staple

Three-Section
Flip Book Template

staple	staple	staple

staple	staple	staple

staple	staple	staple

Four-Section
Flip Book Template

staple	staple	staple	staple

staple	staple	staple	staple

staple	staple	staple	staple